Music and Sound in the Films of Dennis Hopper

Across his directorial films, American filmmaker Dennis Hopper used music and sound to propel the narrative, signpost the era in which the films were made, and delineate the characters' place within American culture. This book explores five of Hopper's films to show how this deep engagement with music to build character and setting continued throughout his career, as Hopper used folk, punk, hip-hop, and jazz to shape the worlds of his films in ways that influenced other filmmakers and foreshadowed the advent of the music video format.

The author traces Hopper's distinctive approach to the use of music through films from 1969 to 1990, including his innovative use of popular rock, pop, and folk in *Easy Rider*, his blending of diegetic performances of folk and Peruvian indigenous music in *The Last Movie*, his use of punk rock in *Out of the Blue*, incorporation of hip-hop and rap in *Colors*, and commissioning of a jazz/blues soundtrack by Miles Davis and John Lee Hooker for *The Hot Spot*. Uncovering the film soundtrack as a vital piece of the narrative, this concise and accessible book offers insights for academic readers in music and film studies, as well as all those interested in Hopper's work.

Stephen Lee Naish is a researcher and writer based in Ontario, Canada.

Filmmakers and Their Soundtracks
Series Editor
James Wierzbicki
The University of Sydney, Australia

Terrence Malick
Sonic Style
James Wierzbicki

Howard Hawks
Music as Communication in Film
Gregory Camp

Music and Sound in the Worlds of Michel Gondry
Kate McQuiston

Music and Sound in the Films of Dennis Hopper
Stephen Lee Naish

For more information about this series, please visit: www.routledge.com/Filmmakers-and-Their-Soundtracks/book-series/FILMSNDTRCK

Music and Sound in the Films of Dennis Hopper

Stephen Lee Naish

NEW YORK AND LONDON

First published 2024
by Routledge
605 Third Avenue, New York, NY 10158

and by Routledge
4 Park Square, Milton Park, Abingdon, Oxon, OX14 4RN

Routledge is an imprint of the Taylor & Francis Group, an informa business

© 2024 Stephen Lee Naish

The right of Stephen Lee Naish to be identified as author of this work has been asserted in accordance with sections 77 and 78 of the Copyright, Designs and Patents Act 1988.

All rights reserved. No part of this book may be reprinted or reproduced or utilised in any form or by any electronic, mechanical, or other means, now known or hereafter invented, including photocopying and recording, or in any information storage or retrieval system, without permission in writing from the publishers.

Trademark notice: Product or corporate names may be trademarks or registered trademarks, and are used only for identification and explanation without intent to infringe.

Library of Congress Cataloging-in-Publication Data
Names: Naish, Stephen Lee, author.
Title: Music and sound in the films of Dennis Hopper / Stephen Lee Naish.
Description: [1.] | New York, NY : Routledge, 2024. | Series: Filmmakers and their soundtracks | Includes bibliographical references and index.
Identifiers: LCCN 2023055516 (print) | LCCN 2023055517 (ebook) | ISBN 9781032737690 (hardback) | ISBN 9781032737683 (paperback) | ISBN 9781003465843 (ebook)
Subjects: LCSH: Hopper, Dennis, 1936–2010—Criticism and interpretation. | Motion picture music—History and criticism. | Popular music in motion pictures. | Film soundtracks—History and criticism.
Classification: LCC ML2075 .N34 2024 (print) | LCC ML2075 (ebook) | DDC 781.5/42—dc23/eng/20231201
LC record available at https://lccn.loc.gov/2023055516
LC ebook record available at https://lccn.loc.gov/2023055517

ISBN: 978-1-032-73769-0 (hbk)
ISBN: 978-1-032-73768-3 (pbk)
ISBN: 978-1-003-46584-3 (ebk)

DOI: 10.4324/9781003465843

Typeset in Times New Roman
by Apex CoVantage, LLC

For J, H, I

Contents

	List of Figures	*viii*
	Series Foreword	*ix*
	Acknowledgments	*xi*
	Introduction: Dennis Hopper in Context	1
1	Keeping It Cool: *Easy Rider,* the Rock Music Compilation Soundtrack, and The Slow Death of the Sixties	10
2	Never-ending Daydream: Diegetic Sound, Aural Assaults, and Folk Mosaics in *The Last Movie* and *The American Dreamer*	24
3	Kill All Hippies: Punk Rock Rebellion, Elvis Presley, and Generational "Burn Out" in *Out of the Blue*	34
4	Rebel Without a Pause: Rap and Hip-Hop's Gang Affiliation, Popularity, and Battle with Authority in *Colors*	44
5	Blue Notes: Jazz and Blues Music Hybridity, and (Mis)Representation of Black Voices in *The Hot Spot*	57
	Conclusion	64
	Bibliography	*71*
	Index	*75*

Figures

1.1	Billy and Wyatt arrive at the small-town parade. This scene foreshadows the more chaotic Mardi Gras Parade they will attend in New Orleans	15
1.2	Billy confronts a Black Mardi Gras festival goer. Despite the rich history of Black music in the South, *Easy Rider* features no prominent Black characters or Black music	17
2.1	Sometimes *The Last Movie*'s visuals and soundtrack converge to create a genuine visual beauty. Here Kansas (Dennis Hopper) and Marie (Stella Garcia) kiss in a meadow with only the sound of the wind	28
2.2	Much like the "acid trip" in *Easy Rider*, the overlapping "in film" audio in *The Last Movie* is designed to be destabilizing and disjointed	29
3.1	Although seemingly untrained Cebe has ambition to be a punk rock star	38
3.2	While wandering the streets of Vancouver, Cebe encounters a street crooner singing an Elvis Presley song	40
4.1	Ice-T's theme song "Colors" intrudes upon the soundtrack when the gang members are rounded up by the cops	49
4.2	A majority of the hip-hop and rap music can be heard playing on stereos in the background when the gangs are hanging out	51
5.1	The rock music that plays in the seedy strip bar on the rundown side of town is the only indication that *The Hot Spot* is a contemporary story	59
5.2	Despite the prominent use of jazz and blues music from two leading Black musicians, the only Black character within the entire film is a blind man	61

Series Foreword

The idea for a series of serious studies of various filmmakers' sonic styles began, as good ideas so often do, with a sidewalk conversation. In this case, the conversation took place during a break between sessions of the Music and the Moving Image conference at New York University in 2011; aside from the fresh air and coffee, its stimulus was the shared observation that since the conference's inception in 2007 there had been a subtle shift in the content of its papers. As one might expect from a conference named the way it is, most of the MaMI papers over the years indeed concentrated on music and its relationship to moving images, usually as demonstrated in singular examples of motion-picture art. But more and more, our sidewalk gang noted, attention was being focused not just on a particular film's music but on *all* its sonic elements, and not just on the sonic elements of a particular film but on the sonic elements of at least a number of films attributed to the same authorial source.

Thus was born *Music, Sound and Filmmakers: Sonic Style in Cinema* (Routledge, 2012), an edited collection whose dozen chapters deal succinctly yet comprehensively with the "stylish" use of sound by the film producers David O. Selznick and Val Lewton and the film directors Wes Anderson, Ingmar Bergman, the Coen brothers, Peter Greenaway, Krzystof Kiéslowski, Stanley Kubrick, David Lynch, Quentin Tarantino, Andrey Tarkovsky, and Gus Van Sant. In my Preface to that edited collection, I noted that "these twelve scholarly essays on sonic style in cinema represent only a first step on what surely will be a long path." A second step along this path, it surely seems, is Routledge's bold decision to follow up with not merely a sequel to the 2012 collection but with a series of monographs.

Contributors to the *Filmmakers and their Soundtracks* series have been charged, as were the contributors to the 2012 collection, with two questions. Can you imagine a situation in which someone, arriving late to a showing of a film about which he or she has no advance information, might spontaneously say: "Ah, that *sounds* like a film by so-and-so?" If such a situation can indeed be imagined, then what is it about the film's sonic content that makes it attributable to one particular filmmaker? Like the essays in *Music, Sound and Filmmakers*, the books in the *Filmmakers and their Soundtracks* series seek to answer that more difficult second question by explaining the many and complex reasons why a filmmaker's work, as a whole, has a distinct sonic "trademark."

James Wierzbicki
Series Editor

Acknowledgments

My gratitude to James Wierzbicki for his dedication, guidance, and support for this project and for founding the series of which this book is part of.

My thanks to the journals and venues that allowed me to write and talk about Dennis Hopper's work and where some of these thoughts originated. Victor Fraga at *Dirty Movies*, Dominic Preston at *Candid Magazine*, Ali Taha at *Archetype*, John Whitehead at *Gadfly*, Marshall Poe at *New Books Network*, Justin Chadwick at *Albumism*, Justin Gage at *Aquarium Drunkard*, Denise Enck at *Empty Mirror*, Liza Palmer at *Film Quarterly*, Joseph Wade at *The Film Magazine*, Jeroen Sondervan at Amsterdam University Press, Rolf Maurer at Newstar Books, and the growers at Hopper Reserve Cannabis. Family: mum, dad, Joanne, Libby, Evie, Brian, Kara, Gail, Ross.

Love to Jamie, Hayden, Isla, and Puff the cat.

Introduction
Dennis Hopper in Context

In the film *Jesus's Son* (1999), the character of F.H. (Billy Crudup) helps Bill, who is played in a small cameo appearance by Dennis Hopper, to wet shave his face. F.H. is residing in the same detox hospital as Bill. As F.H. gently trims away, the two talk about Bill's circumstances. Bill tells F.H. that he has been shot twice in his life "once by each wife." F.H. comments with some surprise: "You're still alive?" To which Bill replies: "Are you kidding? Obviously, I am." F.H. clarifies that what he means is that Bill's life is a kind of miracle. By staring death in the face, not once but twice, Bill should consider himself "alive in a deeper sense." The scene offers a gateway into Hopper's own experiences of artistic triumph and failure as a Hollywood actor, film director, screenwriter, visual artist, and photographer.

Dennis Hopper started his career as a young actor in the mid-1950s contracted to Warner Bros. He appeared in television shows such as *Medic* and *Cheyenne* and became a staple of TV westerns such as *Bonanza* and *Gunsmoke*. His early film roles included small but memorable performances in *Rebel Without a Cause* (1955), *Giant* (1956), and *From Hell to Texas* (1958). His friendship with his *Rebel* and *Giant* costar James Dean influenced his life and acting greatly. Under Dean's guidance, and later with New York-based acting instructor Lee Strasberg, Hopper embraced the "Method" approach to acting in which the performer must exemplify "the external life of his character. He must fit his own human qualities to the life of this person and pour into it all of his own soul."[1] In practice, the performer exists as the character and incorporates the day-to-day mannerisms the character may comprise, using experience and memories drawn from the actor's own life to feed into that of the character's fictional life. As Strasberg wrote: "The extraordinary thing about acting is that life itself is actually used to create artistic results. . . . The actor uses real sensation and real behaviour. That actual reality is the material of our craft."[2]

Hopper's early Hollywood career ended after a series of on-set conflicts with studio bosses and film directors marked him as too difficult to work with. During the early 1960s, he turned his attention to black-and-white still photography and captured the transitional decade as well as his famous friends

DOI: 10.4324/9781003465843-1

and associates. He also became an avid art collector and dabbled in artistic expression. Hopper appeared in small independent films that included the Curtis Harrington-directed *Night Tide* (1961) and *Queen of Blood* (1966), as well as Anthony Lanza's biker exploitation film *The Glory Stompers* (1968). He then positioned himself as a film director in the American New Wave (or New Hollywood) emerging in the late 1960s. Hopper experienced critical and commercial success with his directorial debut *Easy Rider* (1969), in which he also appeared alongside Peter Fonda and Jack Nicholson as bikers traveling across the American West. *Easy Rider* captured and defined the zeitgeist of free love, cultural upheaval, and chemical experimentation just as the decade was winding down.

Thanks to the success of *Easy Rider*, Hopper and Fonda had carte blanche to create whatever projects they desired. Flush with major studio funding, not to mention copious amounts of drugs, Hopper flew to Peru to direct and star in his follow-up feature film *The Last Movie* (1971). At the time, the critical reaction to the film was that it was too abstract and obtuse for mainstream audiences to fully comprehend. The studio executives hated it because they assumed the story of an exploitative movie production company intruding on an indigenous village was criticism of their own moviemaking practices. The critical reaction ostracized Hopper from an already changing Hollywood. The filmgoing public had little opportunity to decide if *The Last Movie* deserved its critical mauling as it was removed from theatrical release after only two weeks of screenings in a number of small cinemas.

Hopper's third directorial film, *Out of the Blue* (1980), dealt with the issues of alcoholism, child abuse, and self-destruction. Critics thought it too harrowing, and audiences of the time stayed away or were again not given the opportunity to see the film for themselves unless a daring movie theater screened it or until the advent of VHS video cassettes, DVD, and – further along the line – online streaming.

After another prolonged spell in the wilderness, Hopper made a triumphant return to acting with three impressive performances, all released in 1986. In David Lynch's dark and menacing *Blue Velvet*, he played the vile sex-crazed gangster Frank Booth. In Tim Hunter's teenage delinquent drama *River's Edge*, he played local weirdo and drug dealer Feck. He played Shooter, the troubled alcoholic coach of a basketball team, in David Anspaugh's drama *Hoosiers*, which would earn Hopper an Oscar nomination for Best Supporting Actor. His reacceptance into mainstream American cinema was assured. Hopper returned reinvigorated and revived and, like Bill in *Jesus's Son*, was shot down twice but alive.

Being "alive in a deeper sense" applies many times to Hopper's acting, directorial, and artistic career. The iconoclast filmmaking days of *Easy Rider*, *The Last Movie*, and *Out of the Blue* are an obvious starting point in understanding this, but there are other moments throughout his career that also reflect this notion.

Critic Adrian Martin described Dennis Hopper as "a prolific, energetic, charismatic performer in A-grade and B-grade films alike, in popular cinema and art cinema, and a ubiquitous, if 'B-list,' media celebrity."[3] Hopper walked the fine line between high art and popular culture. He was celebrated and respected in both mainstream Hollywood movies and underground independent films. He was at home appearing in art-house films such as Sean Penn's *The Indian Runner* (1991) and David Salle's *Search and Destroy* (1995), and comfortable hamming it up in action blockbusters such as *Super Mario Bros.* (1993), *Speed* (1994), and *Waterworld* (1995). These strange contradictions arise repeatedly in Hopper's career.

Hopper's work in film, either as a director or actor, is his most recognized outlet. Yet it is worth noting that all the elements of Hopper's creative life feed into his film work. Through his still photography, he documented the Los Angeles art scene of the early- to mid-1960s. He attended the early art exhibitions of Andy Warhol and Roy Lichtenstein. He captured the lives of his celebrity friends James Brown and Paul Newman, and bands such as The Rolling Stones, as well as the counterculture that surrounded them. He marched from Selma to Montgomery alongside Civil Rights activists and captured the historical gatherings and speeches. His photographs led him to understand framing and composition in preparation for his future directorial work. The spontaneity in these photographs connects to the way he weaved his film camera in and around the action in films such as *Easy Rider* and his fourth directorial film, *Colors* (1988). In his third film, *Out of the Blue*, Hopper used stationary set-ups for his camera in interesting angles and let the actors play out the scenes in long naturalistic takes. Each scene is like a still photograph that comes to life in front of the viewer's eyes.

As an actor and director, Hopper was active from roughly 1955 to a year or so before his death from prostate cancer in 2010. His life and work stretch across historical, cultural, and social movements and events: the Vietnam War and the anti-war movement; the activism of Martin Luther King, Jr., Malcolm X, the Black Panthers, and the triumphs and blows of the Civil Rights movement; the second and third waves of feminism and women's rights; the moon landings, the Summer of Love, and the Monterey Pop and Woodstock Festivals; the presidencies of Eisenhower, Kennedy, Johnson, Nixon, Ford, Carter, Reagan, George H.W. Bush, Clinton, George W. Bush, and Barack Obama; the so-called end of history, the Cold War, and the fall of the Berlin Wall; the terrorist attacks of 11 September and the Bush Administration's War on Terror. Hopper lived through the music of Miles Davis, the Beatles, The Rolling Stones, Bob Dylan, and the Doors. He saw the new wave explosion of the Sex Pistols and the Clash, the rise of pop superstars Madonna and Michael Jackson, and hip-hop and rap artists Tupac Shakur, Public Enemy, and N.W.A., and the grunge rock bands Nirvana and Pearl Jam. He was there for the new movements in art and considered artists such as Bruce Conner, Andy Warhol, Roy Lichtenstein, and Marcel Duchamp as friends. He lived through it all, and his film work reflects this.

Hopper was a significant part of the film industry. He participated in genres of the Western, the epic Hollywood drama, the exploitation film, the early independents, the New Hollywood movement, and the blockbuster movie era. As an actor, he worked alongside James Dean, Marlon Brando, Natalie Wood, Elizabeth Taylor, Dean Martin, John Wayne, Burt Lancaster, Warren Oates, Bruno Ganz, Christopher Walken, Sean Penn, Crispin Glover, Benicio del Toro, Courtney Love, Gary Oldman, Penélope Cruz, and Ben Kingsley, to name but a few. He appeared in films by directors Nicholas Ray, Henry Hathaway, Orson Welles, Roger Corman, Philippe Mora, Wim Wenders, Francis Ford Coppola, Robert Altman, Tobe Hooper, David Lynch, David Salle, Julien Temple, George A. Romero, Isabel Coixet, and many more.

During his film career, Dennis Hopper directed seven features. Along with *Easy Rider*, *The Last Movie*, *Out of the Blue*, and *Colors*, he also directed *Catchfire* (1990), *The Hot Spot* (1990), and *Chasers* (1994). As this book is about soundtracks, the focus will be on the first four of his films and the sixth, *The Hot Spot*. Hopper had a direct hand in conceiving and writing these projects and layering their musical components, whereas in *Catchfire* and *Chasers*, he was more the hired hand steering the film for the studio. This is not to suggest that *Catchfire* or *Chasers* did not adhere to Hopper's vision. In fact, Hopper disowned the studio cut of *Catchfire*, which was released as an "Alan Smithee" film, a term used by directors when a film is taken out of their hands and edited beyond all recognition. Hopper would recut *Catchfire* and re-released it as *Backtrack*. According to filmmaker Michael Almereyda, *Catchfire* and *Chasers*, in comparison to Hopper's earlier work, "showed few traces of conviction or daring." In these films, Almereyda argues, Hopper was "no longer playing for high stakes. It was as if he'd been persuaded that an aggressive personal style was something to run from or hide."[4] Hopper's iconoclasm is most evident in the quartet of *Easy Rider*, *The Last Movie*, *Out of the Blue*, and *Colors*. The passion with which Hopper directed these films is obvious and fierce, and the period's zeitgeist is captured by the music chosen for these films' soundtracks.

Hopper's directorial films never explicitly commented on the eras. Although *Easy Rider* is considered a definitive film of the 1960s and a representation of the hippies and the counterculture, it deals little with the social and political upheaval of that decade. There is no mention of the dying days of the administration of President Lyndon B. Johnson. There is no recognition that Richard Nixon would soon be elected to office, rolling back all the so-called triumphant liberalism of the decade. The ongoing Vietnam War is never hinted at. The radicalization of millions of young people is only witnessed by a small hippie commune. Rather than being representative of a mass event that is supposedly taking place across most of America, the small community of hippies encountered in *Easy Rider* feels like an inconsequential group of middle-class urban escapees. Martin Luther King, Jr., the Black Panthers, Malcolm X, and the Civil Rights Movement are not alluded to. Yet Hopper's use of music does signify the eras in which his films originated. The music placed within *Easy Rider* and the other films does the political and cultural undertaking that narrative progression, dialogue, character development, or *mise-en-scène* might potentially do in another film.

As an actor and as a director, Hopper was never infatuated with the idea of monologues or long exposition dialogue. He relied on gestures, hand movements, spasms of the eyes and lips, and short bursts of (often shouted) dialogue to put across the message. Although it was nominated for an Academy Award for Best Screenplay, the script for *Easy Rider* (which Hopper cowrote with Terry Southern and Peter Fonda), is sparse on dialogue, and only Jack Nicholson's character George Hanson is afforded much time to talk about the culture that surrounds the film. Most of the dialogue is quick-fire prodding to get the narrative moving and vague conversations along the way. When Hopper was given a long, moving monologue to perform – as he was in *Tracks* (1976), in the form of Henry Jaglom's meditation on the damages of the Vietnam War – he threw the pages aside and instead improvised a scene of inarticulate rage and repeated phrases.

Through their soundtracks, Dennis Hopper's directorial films were in a continuous dialogue with one another and bore witness to the demise of the so-called American Dream. This idea will thread itself throughout this book, but a short glance will show that the ideals of personal freedom explored in *Easy Rider* sour toward nihilism and betrayal of that idealism in *Out of the Blue*. The punk rock music used in *Out of the Blue* reacts to the folksy, grandiose rock and folk music of *Easy Rider*. The music creates a striking conversation between one culture and another. The Generation Xers of *Out of the Blue* denounce the Boomers of *Easy Rider* for their lack of follow-through and their willingness to sell out ideals or have those ideals fuse with the mainstream. "Kill all hippies!" is the war cry of *Out of the Blue*'s female protagonist, Cebe Barnes; she means it and, in the end, even goes through with it.

This study will begin with *Easy Rider*. In his first film, Hopper used songs that were rotating on mainstream radio at the time. Included was music by the Jimi Hendrix Experience, Steppenwolf, The Byrds, and Bob Dylan. Alongside material by these superstars of the day, psychedelic oddities by The Electric Prunes and The Holy Modal Rounders also appear. These artists formed a compilation soundtrack where, according to the film's cinematographer, László Kovács, "the music became inseparable from the pictures."[5] The film and its soundtrack captured a moment in the lives of young people in 1960s America unlike what was offered in any other film from that era. The counterculture had never before been represented on film in such a positive way, i.e., people simply going about their business and not being portrayed as antagonistic or violent. *Easy Rider* was a realistic document of its time. The soundtrack that steers the film's two hippie bikers across the southern United States to the cultural mecca of the Mardi Gras festival in New Orleans is one of many elements that give *Easy Rider* its continued cultural relevance. *Easy Rider* gave film soundtracking a new direction. It demonstrated how to use prerecorded and popular songs in film to bolster the visual component by combining lyrics, rhythm, and tone to convey mood and emotion.

Chapter 2 pulls focus on Hopper's second film, *The Last Movie*. As mentioned, the film was a box-office failure and a film that faced a critical mauling at the time of release. The film could be described as an avant-garde metafictional western that shares more with the French New Wave of art-house cinema than with the roaming gunslingers captured in the films of John Ford or Henry Hathaway. Like much of Hopper's work, *The Last Movie* has faced a resurgence of interest. A recent restoration and DVD/Blu-Ray reissue and a vinyl reissue of the soundtrack will be explored within the chapter.

The Last Movie is essentially an avant-garde art-house film given the green light and funding by Hollywood; in this case, Universal Studios. Reaction to *The Last Movie* changed many minds in the top echelons of the studio system. The tried and tested Old Hollywood formula that the auteurs blew out of the water hadn't quite met the standards. A burst of finances and creative control granted to young and hip (and, one should add, inexperienced) directors, producers, actors, screenwriters, and scene setters began to be withdrawn. Although not solely, *The Last Movie* nevertheless helped bring about the slow demise of the New Hollywood era and set the scene for the revival of blockbuster cinematic events such as *Star Wars* and *Jaws*.

The soundtrack of *The Last Movie* will be examined alongside the soundtrack to an accompanying documentary titled *The American Dreamer* (1972). Jointly directed by writer and producer L.M. Kit Carson (writer of *Paris, Texas*) and photojournalist Lawrence Schiller, *The American Dreamer* delves into the postproduction process of *The Last Movie*. It also documents Hopper's increasing instability, chemical addictions, and paranoia, as well as his creative and artistic drive. The soundtracks of both films feature folk compositions from singer/songwriters Kris Kristofferson, Gene Clark, and John Buck Wilkin. Both films also feature a diegetic experimental sound-art component. As the two films are entwined with one another, so are their soundtracks.

Chapter 3 delves into the dark odyssey of Hopper's 1980 feature film *Out of the Blue*. The narrative concerns a female teenage delinquent named Cebe and the return of her abusive father after a five-year spell in prison. Originally only cast to play the role of an alcoholic father in the film, Hopper turned director when the film's original screenwriter and director, Leonard Yakir, exited the production. Hopper chose to rewrite the screenplay and recast some important roles. He also incorporated a spirit of punk rock that was tied to that music's popularity at the time. What is interesting, and what will be explored, is that despite the film being connected to punk rock in the minds of audiences, there is very little punk music within the film. The "punk" attitude is displayed by the ramshackle way in which the film is presented and the confrontational performances by the lead cast members.

Chapter 4 focuses on *Colors*. This was Hopper's first mainstream film after his return to the industry, and the first made clean of drugs, drink, and other vices. There is restraint and a sense of clarity to his direction that complements his newfound sobriety. But there is still an element of danger, and social critique, and Hopper's directorial voice is still clear. *Colors* highlighted the gang culture of urban Los Angeles and the conflicts and hardships faced by Black and Latino youths in the mid-to-late 1980s, especially in relation to the Los Angeles Police Department's Community Resources Against Street Hoodlums (CRASH) units that patrolled and intimidated the residents of gang-controlled neighborhoods. *Colors* differs from previous Hopper directorial efforts in that he did not give himself a prominent role in the film. He instead remained behind the camera and focused solely on the direction of the film. Comparable to how *Easy Rider* incorporated contemporary songs from popular radio stations, *Colors* uses rap and hip-hop music that was immensely popular with Black and Latino youth at the time but had yet to become a mainstream staple of music and culture. *Colors* promoted hip-hop and rap music into the national consciousness.

Chapter 5 concerns Hopper's potboiler neo-noir *The Hot Spot*. Not as well regarded as Hopper's previous works, *The Hot Spot* takes a different approach from Hopper's previous films in that it is essentially a period piece. The film is a pristine caricature of a 1950s American town set in a sweltering summer. Hopper turns his eye to the past but creates a film that says little about either the past or the present. The soundtrack is a fusion of jazz horn, supplied by Miles Davis, with blues guitar and vocal supplied by John Lee Hooker. It breaks with Hopper's soundtracking tradition as it is a commissioned piece of original material recorded especially for the film. Along with Davis and Hooker, an assortment of multi-instrumentalists such as Taj Mahal, Roy Rogers, Earl Palmer, and Tim Drummond join in the fun.

The book's conclusion will attempt to pull on the threads of Hopper's film soundtracks. It will include a discussion of the impact, the triumphs, and the failures of Hopper's involvement with film music.

Before we set upon this journey to discover the nuances of Dennis Hopper's soundtrack work, we should consider what a film soundtrack is and what makes a film soundtrack work. In her book, *Film Music: A Very Short Introduction*, Kathryn Kalinak writes:

> Film music, whether it is a pop song, an improvised accompaniment, or an originally composed cue, can do a variety of things. It can establish setting, specifying a particular time and place; it can fashion a mood and create atmosphere; it can call attention to elements onscreen or offscreen, thus clarifying matters of plot and narrative progression; it can reinforce or foreshadow narrative developments and contribute to the way we respond to them; it can elucidate characters' motivations and help us to know what they are thinking; it can contribute to the creation of emotions, sometimes only dimly realized in the images, both for characters to emote and for audiences to feel. Film music can unify a series of images that might seem disconnected on their own and impart a rhythm to their unfolding. While it is doing all of this, film music encourages our absorption into the film by distracting us from its technological basis.[6]

This descriptor offers the best explanation of what film music is and what it can accomplish. It also applies to Hopper's practice. As will be discussed, Hopper used music to give his films a sense of time and place. Mostly working with contemporary genres, he applied music from the day into his films to place them within the context of the events that his characters were living through.

Hopper's soundtracks harnessed "the power of musical conventions to provide an audible definition of the emotion represented in the film."[7] In addition, his use of songs with lyrics allowed him the "explicit means of transmitting meaning and attention more directly."[8]

Brandon Soderburg noted in his appraisal of Hopper's soundtracking that he acted "like a mash-up artist or genre-spanning DJ," employing "pop music in his films to make unexpected, sympathetic connections between generations – charting changes in youth culture, then putting them in conversation with one another, establishing a continuum of cool."[9] While the image of Hopper working the DJ podium to baying youthful masses might seem ludicrous, there is much truth to the statement. Despite not being youthful as such – Hopper was more than 30 years old when *Easy Rider* landed in movie theaters – Hopper's first four films nevertheless engage with a younger audience through their use of music. It is a credit to Hopper that as he aged and embraced more conservative political points of view he maintained an active interest in the trends of youth culture, and in how these trends were reflected in the music that young people engaged with.

While the focus of this book is Hopper's soundtracks, I cannot ignore, discount, or undermine the films' narratives, performances, and cinematic techniques, the cultural climates that surrounded these films, or the circumstances that brought Hopper to direct them. The soundtracks should be considered complementary to the stories that Hopper's films tell and to the lives and times that they reflect. Hopper used the soundtrack as a narrative tool, and with it, he invited audiences to explore the cultures that his characters inhabited. As I am drawn to all aspects of Hopper's artistic existence, I accept that invitation.

Notes

1 Konstantin Stanislavski, *Stanislavski: An Actor Prepares; Building a Character; Creating a Role* (Abingdon: Taylor & Francis, 1989), 15.
2 Toby Cole and Helen Krich Chinoy, *Actors on Acting: The Theories, Techniques, and Practises of the World's Great Actors, Told in Their Own Words* (New York: Three Rivers Press, 1995), 623.
3 Adrian Martin, "The Misleading Man: Dennis Hopper," in *Stars in Our Eyes: The Star Phenomena in the Contemporary Era*, ed. Angela Ndalianis and Charlotte Henry (Westport: Praeger, 2002), 3–19.
4 Michael Almereyda, "Fade Out: Dennis Hopper," *Film Comment*, July 2010 (available at www.filmcomment.com/article/fade-out-michael-almereyda-on-dennis-hopper/).

5 Frank Mastropolo, "How the Groundbreaking 'Easy Rider' Changed Soundtracks Forever," *Ultimate Classic Rock*, 1 July 2020 (available at https://ultimateclassicrock.com/easy-rider-soundtrack/).
6 Kathryn Kalinak, *Film Music: A Very Short Introduction* (Oxford: Oxford University Press, 2010), 1.
7 Ibid., 19.
8 Ibid., 87.
9 Brandon Soderburg, "Dennis Hopper, Soundtrack Savant: The Unacknowledged Music Savvy Behind *Easy Rider*, *Out of the Blue*, and *Colors*," *The Village Voice*, 1 June 2010 (available at www.villagevoice.com/2010/06/01/dennis-hopper-soundtrack-savant-the-unacknowledged-music-savvy-behind-easy-rider-out-of-the-blue-and-colors/www.villagevoice.com/2010/06/01/dennis-hopper-soundtrack-savant-the-unacknowledged-music-savvy-behind-easy-rider-out-of-the-blue-and-colors/).

1 Keeping It Cool

Easy Rider, the Rock Music Compilation Soundtrack, and The Slow Death of the Sixties

Dennis Hopper's 1969 directorial debut *Easy Rider* was one of the first films in which the soundtrack was compiled from popular songs of the day. It featured late-1960s hard rock standards from Steppenwolf and Jimi Hendrix, and folk music from The Byrds and Bob Dylan, as well as more abstract and psychedelic contributions from The Electric Prunes, The Electric Flag, and The Holy Modal Rounders. The music on the soundtrack steadily builds a mood that mirrors the journey the two hippie bikers, Billy and Wyatt (played by Hopper and Peter Fonda, respectively), take as they drift across the American landscape, chasing down the so-called American Dream (or at least, their interpretation of it) on the custom-built motorcycles they have purchased after a windfall drug deal across the Mexican border.

Billy and Wyatt are America's lost sons. They forsake the stale past and wait for the future to be born while, it should be stated, not actively acknowledging or being seen to participate in any of the radical and progressive movements that defined the 1960s. Billy and Wyatt may have attended the San Francisco love-ins, they may have demonstrated at the anti-war protests that swept across the United States against America's involvement in the Vietnam War, they may have been hip to The Beatles' first televised performance on US television, or even been in attendance at the Monterey Pop Music Festival, Woodstock, or Altamont. They are combinations of cultural identities that existed in 1960s America – the hippie, the peacenik, the bohemian, the outlaw – but they have dropped out and rejected those identities, and therefore have become the misinterpretation of Timothy Leary's "turn on, tune in, drop out" with the less radical "get stoned and abandon all constructive activity."[1]

Any sense of purpose or progress gathered from the decade has been lost to Billy and Wyatt, and because of this, *Easy Rider* makes no great leap to comment on the era of seismic change that it represents. The two companions only goal at this juncture is to get rich quick – which they do by selling cocaine to a wealthy connection played by music producer Phil Spector – buy some good weed for themselves, ride to the Mardi Gras festival in New Orleans, and then, as Billy exclaims just after they hit their windfall, "retire to Florida" to watch

DOI: 10.4324/9781003465843-2

American society make or break itself. They have no interest in the future, the people, or the outcome. They are, as Frederick Douglas put it so eloquently, "men who want crops without plowing up the ground."[2] And, indeed, this very action is undertaken within the film when they spend time at a hippie commune in a rugged mountain sanctuary where the soil is loose, dry, and rocky, and they sense that the commune is "not going to make it."

There are many ways in which *Easy Rider* still resonates all these decades later. Its sense of nostalgia for what is perceived as simpler times is one example of this. The iconic motorcycles keep the film alive among biker communities, outlaw gangs, and motorcycle enthusiasts. The film's gloriously photographed landscapes of America, supplied by cinematographer Lázsló Kovács, make audiences yearn for those vistas. Peter Fonda's immaculate looks and effortless (though slightly vacant) cool is iconic. For a film that takes itself seriously, there is even jocularity to be found, mostly when Jack Nicholson's character George Hanson is on screen. But the film's soundtrack is the most obvious contender as to why *Easy Rider* remains locked in the popular consciousness and is still an object of enjoyment for many, and a source of scholarly intrigue.

Easy Rider brought forth a new dawn in soundtracking. It allowed the up-and-coming crop of young and inexperienced film directors of the American New Wave to place already popular songs into their films to signify character emotion and narrative development in a much broader sense and allow the music itself a visual counterpart. This practice is now commonplace within contemporary film and an audience expectation. For example, try listening to "Stuck in the Middle with You" by Stealers Wheel and not recalling the horrifying ear-cutting scene in Quentin Tarantino's *Reservoir Dogs* (1991), or hearing the slow croon of "The End" by the Doors without recalling images of the Vietnam jungle in flames as seen in Francis Ford Coppola's *Apocalypse Now* (1977). The opening credit sequence of *Mean Streets* (1973), soundtracked by "Be My Baby" by the Ronettes, gives a sense of energy that does not let up for the rest of the film. Iggy and the Stooges' swaggering punk rock classic "Lust for Life," as used in Danny Boyle's *Trainspotting* (1996), instantly invokes the image of two wire-thin shoplifters charging down a city street with the police in pursuit.

By using popular musical standards, Hopper and those directors who have followed in his footsteps have placed audio signifiers within their films that give the film gravitas or just make them immensely fun or extremely harrowing to watch.

This is especially apparent in *Easy Rider*'s most notable song. Steppenwolf's "Born to Be Wild" conjures up images of the blazing desert road of the American South, the dirty blast of hot exhaust air, the noise, and speed of the motorcycle engines, and the smell of hot leather and engine oil. Like much of the rest of the soundtrack, "Born to Be Wild" is forever connected to *Easy Rider*'s visual style.

It was all an accident of time and place. Hopper's relationship with the key players of the 1960s counterculture and the music scene (Bob Dylan, members of The Rolling Stones, and Neil Young were some of Hopper's close associates at the time), and his knowledge of trends in popular music, greatly influenced his career as a film director. His use of music within his own directorial films generated cultural markers that offered commentary on the films' fictional narratives and the factual events that surround the eras in which the films were made. When Hopper incorporated rock and folk songs from the 1960s into the soundtrack of *Easy Rider*'s jaunt, the songs not only provided an entertaining visual and aural experience but also added significance to the narrative. Hopper and the film's official editor Donn Cambern (the editorial process was complicated with actor Jack Nicholson and film director Henry Jaglom both attempting to cut down Hopper's original four-hour cut) initially used the music to create a rough draft and to give the film a rhythm that could then be replicated by the musicians that would provide an original score. As Cambern explained in an article for the film's fiftieth anniversary: "We kept listening and culling, and listening and culling, and finally getting to the point where we had really worked out, over a long period of time, the music that we felt would be appropriate."[3]

The intention had been for an original soundtrack to be recorded by folk-rock superstars Crosby, Stills, and Nash. However, according to Hopper, the group's celebrity and excesses did not gel with his own and with the perspective that *Easy Rider* was trying to take. As Hopper explained:

> I had a falling out with Stephen Stills. We were driving back to my office in his limo and I said, 'Stephen, this simply isn't going to work.' He asked why and I shouted, 'Because I've never been in a limo before and anyone who drives around town in a limo can't understand my movie!'[4]

This dramatic disagreement led *Easy Rider* to become a milestone in film soundtracking. Before *Easy Rider*, it was virtually unheard of for a movie to use preexisting music by popular bands and artists. The norm was for a film to be scored by a set of composers or session musicians after an initial edit of the movie had become available, but *Easy Rider* "opened that whole conception of thinking that a song really needs to be placed for its narrative value, as well as its playability in a scene – that is, its contribution."[5]

It was not the first film to place preexisting music in the soundtrack. *Blackboard Jungle* (1955) used "Rock Around the Clock" by Bill Haley and His Comets as its opening motif, and elements of the song were heard throughout the film. As the 1960s progressed, several films featured original folk-rock scores recorded predominantly by one artist. In the case of *The Graduate* (1967), folk duo Simon and Garfunkel provided original compositions that made up the bulk of the soundtrack material.

Music-centered films such as the Beatles' *A Hard Day's Night* (1964), *Yellow Submarine* (1968), and the Monkees' film *Head* (1968), had used musical performances and recordings by the featured bands as a narrative tool. These films acknowledged the music on the soundtrack by using performances of the songs by the cast. The music in films such as *The Graduate* and *Easy Rider* was non-diegetic and told the audience of the "protagonist's alienation"[6] through lyrical connections the characters could not hear themselves.

Alongside the aforementioned music-oriented films, *Easy Rider* also functioned as a prelude to the creation of the music video format that would be the basis for music channels such as MTV and VH1 in the mid-1980s. It is certainly easy to identify the embryonic music-video style of quick-fire editing and the use of symbolism or metaphor to tell a short narrative in the absence of any dialogue. According to Andrew Goodwin in his book *Dancing in the Distraction Factory*, this process of film soundtracking leading toward music videos was a natural evolution: "In its earliest days rock and roll was promoted via film; indeed, many teens first discovered rock at the movies."[7] Today, music incorporates film language via a promotional music video to promote a song and send it up the charts.

Steppenwolf's "The Pusher" is the first song we hear on the soundtrack. It is a sullen and moody start to proceedings. The song deplores the role of the drug pusher in American countercultural society by calling him a "monster" who doesn't care if their consumer lives or dies. The song plays while Wyatt is threading cash from the cross-border drug sale into the gas tank of his custom-built motorcycle. Billy and Wyatt are not drug pushers; they have stumbled into a drug deal, and this is made clear within the song when Steppenwolf proclaims that the dealer sells "sweet dreams," while the pusher is not a "natural man." The dealer and the pusher are different, but despite this difference, the drug deal still fuels the cross-border drug market and will continue the negative role of the drug pusher on society for many decades to come.

"The Pusher" is a slow yet urgent composition, but Steppenwolf's second contribution to the film, "Born to Be Wild," is the song that has become synonymous with *Easy Rider*. An "explosive pairing of image and sound,"[8] the scene that features the song is really where the narrative begins. The chugging rhythm, driving guitar lines, and distorted squalls sound like the rattling engines of Billy's and Wyatt's bikes as they ride on the sun-boiled asphalt. The lyrical content also, at least on the surface, matches up with the journey as they hit the highway and embrace the possibilities of the open road. Steppenwolf's anthem of freedom has an emphasis on the "we," and it attempts to convey a mood of collective freedom. In this case, only Billy and Wyatt, not their generation, have freed themselves from the shackles of society. It is clear by their intentions to leave society behind that they both no longer believe in collectivism but only in individual freedom.

The suggestion that "Born to Be Wild" is a song for a generational shift in consciousness was put to rest decades later by Hopper himself as he, middle-aged at this point, clean-shaven and with neat hair and smart attire, met up, with the help of green-screen technology, with *Easy Rider*'s Billy for a 1998 television advertising campaign for the Ford Cougar car. In the advert, the present-day Hopper encounters his younger self on the road, and the two share a cup of coffee at a roadside diner before the present-day Hopper hits accelerate in his Cougar and leaves his former self choking in the dust. The use of "Born to Be Wild" as the soundtrack to the Cougar advertisement diminished the song's countercultural credibility and, indeed, brought into question *Easy Rider*'s anti-commercialism stance; instead of trying to sell the idea of an alternative lifestyle, now *Easy Rider* was being used to entice Baby Boomer consumers to purchase a sensible car.

The musical interludes of *Easy Rider* provide mosaics of cinematic imagery that complement the various songs and underline their meaning within the film. Hopper's directorial work has a tendency to emphasize narratives by means of lyrical accompaniment. For example, the imagery for The Byrds' psychedelic folk standard "I Wasn't Born to Follow" shows Billy and Wyatt gliding through a gorgeous sunlit forest, then into a deep valley that runs off into the horizon, the sunlight creates flashes of lens flare against Kovács's film camera. The montage of images is mirrored by the song's harmonies and by its lyrical content that describes the "valleys," the "cascading waters," the "forests," that the highways run through, and makes reference to a "sacred mountain." where a spiritual awakening occurs. To further emphasize the lyrics, Billy and Wyatt pull up to a gas station called The Sacred Mountain. The imagery of the film corresponds with and complements the lyrical content of "I Wasn't Born to Follow," and vice versa.

The song returns later in the film as Billy and Wyatt are joined by two women from a hippie commune for an idyllic swim in a nearby "legendary fountain." They chance upon this commune when they pick up a lone male hitchhiker (Luke Askew), who appears to be on the same spiritually aligned journey as Billy and Wyatt. Although he is quiet and reveals little about himself to the two bikers, he does reluctantly disclose that he is "from a city, a long way from a city, and that's where I want to be right now." Like Billy and Wyatt, the hitchhiker has dropped out of society, but he remains interested in communal good, and he directs the two toward a hippie commune he is establishing.

Although we know very little about the hitchhiker, the song that accompanies his journey is telling of his circumstances. The Band's performance of their song "The Weight" plays over another montage of road and bike imagery. The song, perhaps more so than "Born to Be Wild," illustrates the nature of being on the road and trying to find a place to "hide" from the world and to find a bed where the weary wanderer can rest. The song's gentle beat and plodding piano give it momentum and a sense of space that wonderfully marries with the images of the three men gliding across the rugged desert landscape. One moment seems to twin audio and visual perfectly. As the hitchhiker points to the distance, Billy follows his arm, and Kovács pulls the camera out wider, which allows Billy to, in effect, push the frame out, and suddenly the wide landscape comes into view. The significance of "The Weight" has to do with the fact that Billy and Wyatt have taken on the weight of the hitchhiker, not just his physical self and his travel bags but also his cultural baggage. The hitchhiker represents an avenue that they have discounted. Although alone, he is traveling toward a hippie commune to find kinship with his fellow men and women. As the song ends, a peaceful and sustained wind sweeps in, and the three men climb a rock formation in Arizona's Monument Valley to watch a blissful sunset. There are not many moments within the film that allow the characters, as well as the audience a chance to breathe, but this is one of them.

While there is often great meaning contained in the soundtrack and its running commentary on the action, there are also moments that apply light comical relief yet still complement the film's narrative flow. Songs such as Fraternity of Man's reefer anthem "Don't Bogart Me" and The Holy Modal Rounders' bizarre and joyous "If You Want to Be a Bird" accompany humorous scenes, and they offer a lightness of touch and an opportunity for the soundtrack to showcase another side of sixties music.

Billy and Wyatt arrive in a small southern town and are locked up in jail for joining in a local parade "without a permit." The sound of cheers and a marching band is a foreshadowing of when the two bikers will arrive in New Orleans later on. Here the music is loud yet practiced; the sounds they encounter in New Orleans will be similar, but far more chaotic and improvised. In the town's jail, they meet George Hanson (Jack Nicholson), a Southern lawyer with liberal leanings who tells them he has "done a lot of work for the ACLU." George negotiates the release of Billy and Wyatt and decides to join them on the road to New Orleans so that he can drink and party at a bordello he has heard about from a friend. When they first hit the road, The Holy Modal Rounders' "If

Figure 1.1 Billy and Wyatt arrive at the small-town parade. This scene foreshadows the more chaotic Mardi Gras Parade they will attend in New Orleans.

Source: *Easy Rider*

You Want to Be a Bird" jumps into the cut and we see the three men joyfully pulling stunts on the bikes and laughing. The song signifies Hanson's newfound freedom (he is now "free as a bird") of leaving his hometown behind and embracing new ideas. When the three of them settle down for the evening we are again treated to a moment of calm and conversation; under the loose (and very stoned) talk about aliens, only the sound of crickets chirping can be heard.

The morning after this night of reefer madness, during which George inhales marijuana for the first time and becomes instantly hooked, we hear Fraternity of Man's "Don't Bogart Me" shimmer in with its laid-back guitar groove as the three men continue their journey. In contrast to the previous day's ride, where excitement was felt at the new possibilities of the road, George, now sold on the weed, is shown crashed out in the passenger seat in a contented post-marijuana nap. Billy and Wyatt have not held back the joint and have indeed, for good or bad, passed the joint over to their new companion. "It was," as editor Donn Cambern explained about the use of the song, "a continuum of a good feeling, of discovery of the land they were going through."[9]

This wonderful land of discovery is abruptly cut into by Jimi Hendrix's jarring guitar line intro to "If 6 Were 9" and the forested, mountainous, and expansive landscapes that Billy and Wyatt have traversed are suddenly replaced by the man-made structure of Louisiana's Long-Allen Bridge. This change in scenery signifies the sense of unease that hangs over the second half of *Easy Rider* as the group enters the deep Southern states. The first half of the film glides on an air of carefree adventurism, and the musical choices have for the most part symbolized this freewheeling approach. The second half of the film is where the characters pay the price for their actions and ideology (or lack thereof), and the mood, in both visual and musical compositions, is severely darkened.

As Little Eva's "Let's Turkey Trot" plays on the radio inside a roadside diner, the three men are subjected to a barrage of insults and threats by a group of tough-looking men. A group of giggling teenage girls take lustful interest in the strangers. The three men eventually leave the diner without getting service. They take up camp a few miles down the road and around the campfire and discuss the downfall of American society and how freedom, once the outlining goal of the American Dream, is something that now scares many people. Hanson states that "this used to be one helluva good country," which has a similar notion to Ronald Reagan's and Donald Trump's campaign slogans that expressed the idea of looking back to an almost fictional past and state of American exceptionalism and values. As the fire dies out and the three travelers turn in for the night, the men from the diner appear and bludgeon George to death with baseball bats. In this case, the men did not kill the long-haired hippies who they hate but went after their own for the betrayal that they believe is worse. George's death scene, filmed in almost complete darkness, is not cut to a jolting crash of instruments of the sort that might be used in a lesser film to create a feeling of tension or disturbance; instead, the only sound is that of blunt sticks beating against a human body. It is a stark moment in a film that has thus far used music to emphasize its visual narrative. The audience might well expect music here, but there is none to be heard.

Easy Rider's sense of uneasiness continues. After Hendrix's "If 6 Were 9" dramatically changes the film's mood there is no turning back, and the story continues with Billy and Wyatt arriving in New Orleans and visiting the House of Blue Lights bordello that George had recommended to them. Across the soundtrack, The Electric Prunes' discordant "Kyrie Eleison Mardis Gras (When the Saints)" is repeatedly cut into by Billy's justification to Wyatt for spending the evening with the sex workers and consuming with gusto a "groovy" dinner. "Kyrie Eleison" sustains the uneasy mood with its chanted mantra before a distorted electric guitar sends the composition into an orgasmic seizure of riffing guitars and crashing drums that marks the transition into the street scene that comes next.

Billy and Wyatt, accompanied by Karen and Mary, two of the sex workers from the bordello (Karen Black and Toni Basil, respectively), head out into the bustling street. Here, Hopper uses only the diegetic sound of the street performers, incorporating and overlapping a soulful yet frantic performance of "When the Saints Go Marching In" with voices of revelers and distant police sirens. The "found sound" aspect gives this portion of the film an improvisational and chaotic feel, and it serves as a prelude to the infamous scene that shows Billy, Wyatt, Karen, and Mary splitting an acid tab and tripping out in New

Figure 1.2 Billy confronts a Black Mardi Gras festival goer. Despite the rich history of Black music in the South, *Easy Rider* features no prominent Black characters or Black music.

Source: *Easy Rider*

Orleans' St. Louis Cemetery No. 1. As Daniel J. Schneider has noted, the scene interrupts *Easy Rider*'s relatively calm and carefree narrative with "super-fast edits, jarring sound effects, Catholic prayers and shots of the Virgin Mary" in an "attempt to replicate the sensation of a 'bad trip.'"[10] Within this scene, the metallic beat of an oil extractor machine continues its clanging rhythm as the street performance fades out. Over the throbbing racket, snippets of dialogue can only just be heard, with Wyatt pleading and whimpering while seated on a statue of the Madonna about the suicide of his mother. As will be discussed in the next chapter, this one scene would greatly influence Hopper's next directorial effort, *The Last Movie*, which used a mix of diegetic sound and live performance throughout to create a similar but much longer disorientating feeling.

The trip scene abruptly cuts to Billy and Wyatt riding away from New Orleans and continuing their journey toward Florida. The surrounding landscape is still industrial, with thick smog blocking out the sun and choking the road ahead. The accompanying music is the psychedelic instrumental "Flash, Bam, Pow" by the rock-blues outfit The Electric Flag, and it links *Easy Rider* with an earlier film – *The Trip* (1967), written by Jack Nicholson and directed by Roger Corman – in which Hopper and Fonda both appeared. *The Trip* concerns Paul (Fonda), a director of television commercials, experimenting with acid for the first time. The film's soundtrack, including "Flash, Bam, Pow," was performed by The Electric Flag. Hopper had had some directorial experience on *The Trip*, shooting as second unit director a nighttime scene in which Paul wanders the city and is bombarded by "neon signs, storefront advertising, billboards, music pouring out of discos, and motor traffic" in what would be an "early instance of the combination of photography, music, and editing that would make *Easy Rider* so potent."[11] The use of "Flash, Bam, Pow" in *Easy Rider* hints at what the film might have been if its soundtrack had been entirely composed by session musicians, and it is unlike the previous scenes of Billy and Wyatt traversing the landscape accompanied by emotive songs that offer insight into the characters' internal thoughts and feelings. This short scene is mostly forgettable, but coming as it does after the aural and visual assault of the graveyard trip scene, it serves as a palate cleanser for what comes next.

For *Easy Rider* to fully comprehend the cultural shifts of the 1960s it was inevitable that its soundtrack should include one of the era's most recognizable voices: Bob Dylan. The last two songs on the soundtrack – "It's Alright, Ma (I'm Only Bleeding)" and "The Ballad of Easy Rider" – were both written by Dylan, but due to Fonda being unable to secure the rights to Dylan's original recordings both were re-recorded for the soundtrack by Byrds front man Roger McGuinn. "It's Alright, Ma (I'm Only Bleeding)" was originally recorded for Dylan's 1965 album *Bringing It All Back Home*. "The Ballad of Easy Rider," on the other hand, was an original composition that Dylan had scribbled down after seeing a rough-cut version of the film.

"It's Alright, Ma" contains apocalyptic imagery that signifies not only Billy and Wyatt's pending demise but also the generational collapse and death of the

1960s' utopian ideology. The lyrics conjure "tormented imagery" that concerns "war, hypocrisy and consumerism,"[12] the song articulates the already wavering ideals that *Easy Rider* predicts would soon end. This is most obvious in the film's final campfire scene, in which the two friends seem incredibly distant from one another and, despite achieving all they had set out to do, Wyatt solemnly comments to Billy that they "blew it."

Wyatt's comment has been dissected countless times as one that contains a multitude of meanings. One angle suggests that the two friends blew their chance at finding community and happiness with their fellow men and women. Indeed, there are several encounters that Wyatt has along the journey that point to his yearning for being a part of something bigger than his current escapade with Billy. An early scene with a farmer who helps them mend a blown tire and then invites them to join him and his large family for dinner impresses Wyatt; it is obvious he envies the position the farmer is in as a man who can "live off the land" and do "his own thing in his own time." The fleeting time spent with the hitchhiker and the hippies is another moment in which Wyatt seems impressed with the efforts they are making to create a sustainable commune; Billy scoffs at Wyatt's comment that the commune is "gonna make it," meaning that they will grow their own food in the barren landscape and live off the land, but the hitchhiker actually offers Wyatt an opportunity to stay at the commune, saying that "this could be the place" that he has been trying to find. These encounters always leave Billy agitated or hostile to those around him. He mocks the hitchhiker's use of the phrase "be a trifle polite" when advocating for respect for the indigenous land they occupy. When Wyatt listens to the hitchhiker's invitation for them to stay with the commune, Billy loudly exclaims, "Hey! If we're goin,' we're goin'! Let's go!" Later he openly threatens George when he makes a wild racket in their shared jail cell. As the farmer and his family say grace at the dinner table, Billy looks amused and on the verge of laughter. It is as if Billy knows that his companion is just one good offer away from leaving him behind and so "plays gravedigger to their hopes and aspirations."[13] Wyatt's comment of "we blew it" could really be aimed at himself and his lack of drive or unwillingness to disappoint his companion.

Another perspective, and the one that gains the most traction, has it that the "we" in "we blew it" is really the entire generation and the utopian ideals that seemed only a short leap away, but which instead were sold out or incorporated into the mainstream and diluted. As Ivan Salinas points out in his retrospective of *Easy Rider*, "the tumultuous '60s ended on a note that said the status quo would remain and be reinforced."[14] The 1960s generation had the opportunity to create a new way of thinking and a new way of existing, at least from the perspective of the culturally powerful United States; instead, the majority caved and conformed to normality.

As Billy and Wyatt continue their journey back out into the American heartlands, they are passed by two locals in a pick-up truck who point a shotgun at them in an attempt to scare them away. Billy gives the two men the middle finger. The gun accidentally goes off. Billy skids off his bike and into a ditch at the side of the road. Wyatt doubles back to help his friend. Wyatt covers Billy with his jacket and leaves to get help. The two locals swing back around and shoot Wyatt. The film ends with both Billy and Wyatt dead by the side of the road and their motorcycles in flames.

Bob Dylan's "The Ballad of Easy Rider," again performed on the soundtrack by McGuinn, quietly builds as the camera hovers higher and higher above the wreckage of the two burning bikes. "The Ballad of Easy Rider" is the only composition written specifically for the film and with direct reference to the circumstances of its narrative. The first line of the song corresponds to the images on the screen of a wide and rushing river that "flows" out to the sea. In the *Easy Rider* "making of" documentary *Shaking the Cage* (1999), Fonda indicates that this shot was purposeful in showing the "road that man built and the road that God built."

Later in the song, Dylan's lyric echoes the conversation about personal freedom that Billy, Wyatt, and George had around the campfire earlier in the film, stating that all our protagonists wanted was to be "free" and that death has become the only true freedom they will ever know. The line also suggests that in order to become free – in order to avoid Billy and Wyatt's fate – the entire counterculture had to sell out, have their experiences co-opted, and compromise on ideals.

A negative aspect of the soundtrack concerns its overall "whiteness" and the overall "maleness" of the artists and groups included; Jimi Hendrix's "If 6 Were 9" represents the soundtrack's only African American voice. Despite the film taking place over the expanse of the American South, where the rich cultural and musical heritage of African American blues, soul, and jazz is prominent, these genres are mostly absent from the film.

The soundtrack reflects the whiteness of *Easy Rider*'s cast and crew. A Black presence is only felt during the New Orleans Mardi Gras scene where Black street performers rattle through their rendition of "When the Saints Go Marching In" and when Billy has a tense stand-off with a Black festival attendee. There are also a few Black Americans appearing on the side of the road, wringing out laundry outside their rundown shacks. No prominent Black figure is featured in the ensemble of members of the hippie commune that Billy and Wyatt visit. Despite the progress of the American Civil Rights movement during the 1960s, and despite Hopper's photographic documentation of the Civil Rights protests and of Martin Luther King, Jr., as he marched from Selma to Montgomery, Black activism and Black culture are virtually absent in both the visual and the audio content of *Easy Rider*.

Female recording artists are also, for the most part, absent from the soundtrack. A female backing vocal can be heard on "Don't Bogart Me," and female singer-songwriter Carole King is credited for writing "I Wasn't Born to Follow." This is surprising when one considers the wealth of prominent female artists of the time that included Janis Joplin, Joni Mitchell, Tina Turner, Nina

Simone, Grace Slick of Jefferson Airplane, The Ronettes, and Cass Elliot and Michelle Phillips of The Mamas and the Papas. But it matches the representation of women within the film itself. When they do appear, women are timid homekeepers, promiscuous lovers, or scantily clad sex workers. The women's liberation movement of the 1960s is on pause in the world of *Easy Rider*. While the males attend to the business of organizing their own "personal freedom" and disconnecting from civil society at large, women shoulder the burden of keeping the homestead functioning. This is notable in the commune scene in which the organizational duties are performed mostly by Sarah (Sabrina Scharf) as her partner, the hitchhiker, rambles around the country and then sheepishly returns to resume control of the commune.

To speculate: Perhaps Hopper decided to depict these groups as marginalized because he knew that – even though women's liberation existed, and the end of racial segregation had occurred through legislation – there was still much action to take before these groups would make an impact on society in a notable way. It was very much a male-dominated decade, and it was very much a *white* male-dominated decade. This, of course, is open to interpretation. *Easy Rider* could have contained the advances and collaboration of the women's movement and the work of the Black liberation movement. But Hopper chose not to do this, and therefore planted the film's flag firmly.

Despite *Easy Rider* being concerned with the white male perspective of its protagonists, the film does not paint the male figure in any particularly positive light. Billy and Wyatt are irresponsible dreamers; George Hanson, although holding down a job as a lawyer, is a terrible drunk and misogynist; the hitchhiker whom they pick up and take to the hippie commune is a flake who comes and goes out of his commune at will. Women might not have representation in *Easy Rider*'s narrative or soundtrack, but the females featured seem a lot hipper and more together than the roaming males that the film focuses on.

It was doubtless always going to be this way. The idea of *Easy Rider* was dreamt up by Fonda in a marijuana haze while pondering a promotional still from the set of Roger Corman's *The Wild Angels* (1966), in which Fonda has the leading role alongside Nancy Sinatra. The photograph in question depicts Fonda in shades and dressed in an all-black leather jacket and jeans, pulling on the final dregs of a cigarette while straddling his motorcycle. It is the very definition of male-loner "cool" and Fonda adapted his *Wild Angels* persona to *Easy Rider*'s Wyatt without many esthetic changes to the overall look.

Easy Rider was just the beginning of this trend in what we might term masculine yearning, a longing for something beyond the ordinary. Hopper's characters have an infinity for being loners and for looking toward a version of personal freedom that is unique to them. These are characteristics Hopper himself took into his acting roles, but they also apply to his directorial output, and his soundtracks make this yearning explicit.

All three of *Easy Rider*'s main stars had come from the late 1960s factory of fear-mongering biker films. Fonda starred in *The Wild Angels*; Nicholson appeared in *Hells Angels on Wheels* (1967), and Hopper appeared in *The Glory Stompers* (1967), which, if Hopper is to be believed, could be credited as his unofficial directorial debut since the film's actual director, Anthony M. Lanza jumped ship early on in the film's production and left Hopper to finish the picture.[15]

These early films featuring *Easy Rider*'s main actors shared several common threads: They were cheap, exploitative, quickly shot, and edited. All three films had generic soundtracks of psychedelic-style instrumental rock music that did nothing to further their narratives or speak to the internal thoughts of the characters. *Easy Rider*, despite having its origins in these cheap biker flicks, is far superior. The visual style of cinematographer László Kovács helps give the film an epic quality. But it is the musical accompaniment that really steers the film toward something more monumental and far reaching.

Despite the glaring faults discussed above, the soundtrack of *Easy Rider* is an important artifact of the times. As a compilation record, it is a solid, if incomplete, snapshot of an era of radical and progressive change. It is an eclectic mix of rock, folk, and psychedelic music that otherwise might have drifted into obscurity had they not been spliced onto a narrative and collection of visuals that have become iconic not just in the realm of film but within popular culture itself. As we turn toward the other films that Dennis Hopper directed, it will become apparent that *Easy Rider*, a film that Hopper continually referenced and made comparisons to, hangs like the Sword of Damocles over the rest of his career. With *Easy Rider*, Hopper became what Adrian Martin terms "indelibly associated" with the 1960s and with its counterculture; his persona became "mythologized, de-mythologized, and re-mythologized by the mass media," and his career thereafter became a "perpetual reenactment of the decade."[16]

Whether this was a blessing or a curse matters little. *Easy Rider* and its soundtrack are a perfect symbiont. Each might have existed without the other in lesser states, but together they came alive.

Notes

1 Timothy Leary, *Flashbacks Personal and Cultural History of an Era* (Los Angeles: J.P. Tarcher, 1990), 253.
2 Frederick May Holland, *Frederick Douglass: The Colored Orator* (New York: Haskell House, 1969), 261.
3 Tim Greiving, "*Easy Rider* at 50: How Groundbreaking Soundtrack Came Together," *Los Angeles Times*, 11 August 2019 (available at www.latimes.com/entertainment-arts/movies/story/2019-08-09/easy-rider-at-50-how-they-put-together-that-groundbreaking-soundtrack).
4 Richard Luck, "A Reefer Runs Through It: The Making of *Easy Rider*," *Sabotage Times*, 20 November 2013 (available at http://sabotagetimes.com/reportage/a-reefer-runs-through-it-the-making-of-easy-rider/).

5 Greiving, "*Easy Rider* at 50."
6 Frank Mastropolo, "How the Groundbreaking *Easy Rider* Changed Soundtracks Forever," *Ultimate Classic Rock*, 1 July 2020 (available at https://ultimateclassicrock.com/easy-rider-soundtrack/).
7 Andrew Goodwin, *Dancing in the Distraction Factory: Music Television and Popular Culture* (Minneapolis: University of Minnesota Press, 1992), 8.
8 Mastropolo, "How the Groundbreaking *Easy Rider* Changed Soundtracks Forever."
9 Greiving, "*Easy Rider* at 50."
10 Daniel Schneider, "Convention Defiance in Dennis Hopper's *Easy Rider*," *Pop Matters*, 3 June 2010 (available at www.popmatters.com/dennis-hopper-easy-rider-defiance).
11 Lee Hill, *Easy Rider* (London: BFI Publishing, 1996), 13.
12 Iain Colley, *Film Notes: "Easy Rider"* (London: Longman, 2000), 52.
13 Jean-Baptiste Thoret, "Dennis/Hopper, or the Man Who Was Two and One," in *Dennis Hopper & the New Hollywood,* ed. Matthieu Orlean (Paris: Flammarion, 2010), 62–67.
14 Ivan Salinas, "Easy Rider' in 2020: Born to Be Dead," *Daily Sundial*, 25 January 2020 (available at https://sundial.csun.edu/156233/arts-entertainment/easy-rider-in-2020-born-to-be-dead/).
15 Interview with Quentin Tarantino conducted by Dennis Hopper, "Blood Lust Snicker Snicker in Widescreen," in *Dennis Hopper: Interviews*, ed. Nick Dawson (Jackson: University Press of Mississippi, 2012), 153–61.
16 Adrian Martin, "The Misleading Man: Dennis Hopper," in *Stars in Our Eyes. The Star Phenomena in the Contemporary Era*, ed. Angela Ndalianis and Charlotte Henry (Westport: Praeger, 2002), 3–19.

2 Never-ending Daydream
Diegetic Sound, Aural Assaults, and Folk Mosaics in *The Last Movie* and *The American Dreamer*

Easy Rider provided audiences with a chronicle of 1960s America without directly commenting on the triumphs and failures of the radical and progressive movements that had occurred. The film's critical adoration and box-office success made Dennis Hopper and Peter Fonda cultural icons and gave them freedom to pursue their filmmaking interests. Hopper and Fonda were not the only actors and auteur film directors to launch themselves into the new movie-making environment they had inadvertently manufactured. The films that came out of the New Hollywood era are best categorized as "independently financed, low-budget films, made by non-studio-trained directors, who combined highly personal or politically radical stories that broke with conventional Hollywood narrative techniques while borrowing heavily from the respective styles of New Wave, cinéma vérité, and avant-garde films."[1] A definitive list of what is considered a New Hollywood film is open to debate, but it's safe to assume that *Easy Rider*, while certainly one of the most successful and recognizable entries, did not start the movement. Films such as *Mickey One* (1965), *Bonnie and Clyde* (1967), *The Graduate* (1967), and *Alice's Restaurant* (1969) came before *Easy Rider* and were made with moderate budgets, contained eccentric performances, and used varied cinematic techniques and were critically acclaimed and reasonably successful. Film actor and director John Cassavetes had been directing small, improvisational, and self-funded films such as *Shadows* (1959) and *Faces* (1968) in the decade leading up to the release of *Easy Rider*. *Easy Rider* was not entirely new, yet with its striking cinematography and soundtrack it connected with the cultural zeitgeist of the time.

Easy Rider's distributors, Universal Studios, gave Hopper and Fonda each a million-dollar budget and creative control of their next film projects. Universal desired follow-ups to *Easy Rider* from both its stars – films that would speak to and define the dreams and aspirations of the previous decade. Peter Fonda directed and starred in *The Hired Hand* (1971), a slow-burning revisionist western in which he portrayed a wandering cowboy returning home to his wife after several years away from the homestead. Hopper wanted to go much further than the hints of social analysis seen in *Easy Rider*. He wanted to aim a critique at the heart of the movie business and American culture at large. He took Universal's money and his entourage of actors – including Peter Fonda, Dean Stockwell, and Russ Tamblyn – as well as his friends and associates, drug dealers, and hangers-on into the mountains of Peru to begin production on *The Last Movie*, a story that dealt with the "destructive potential of American movies"[2] on the indigenous peoples of the Chinchero region and with the last remaining film crew member who stays behind to exploit the region for future film production but instead falls victim to his own personal demons and becomes a pariah to the indigenous population.

Hopper had envisioned *The Last Movie* as being his first directorial work. A few years before *Easy Rider*, Hopper, and screenwriter Stewart Stern had concocted the screenplay in a number of marijuana-infused writing sessions. The two had met a decade previously when Hopper was cast in a supporting role in Nicholas Ray's *Rebel Without a Cause* (1955). Stern had been the chief screenwriter of that film. Working from a story Hopper had overheard on the set of the western *The Sons of Katie Elder* (1965), they wrote a relatively straightforward screenplay. The film might have remained steady if Hopper had been given the green light to direct *The Last Movie* sometime in the late 1960s. But after the success of *Easy Rider*, and in awe of his own self-mythologizing, Hopper developed a very different perspective of what the new film would become. During the production process, the screenplay was cast aside to allow the actors room for improvisation. In post-production, the film was edited into a nonlinear form, reducing parts of the story that Stern's script had focused on to background narratives. The completed film strayed so far from the original screenplay that Stern felt it was not "an accurate representation" of the script he and Hopper had written; he complained that Hopper had not used "the scenes as they were written in the screenplay" and that "he chose to improvise with people who were not up to that kind of improvisation."[3] From on-set reportage at the time and reminiscences from the cast and crew decades later, one can assume that the consumption of drugs and alcohol and the participation in debauchery and self-aggrandizing played a part in the film going off script. Hopper seemed to be aiming for notoriety, political and social commentary, and artistic merit in place of entertainment for the cinema-going public. The aim for the film was to antagonize the audience and make them confront uncomfortable truths about American culture, colonization, and exploitation. This antagonism can be witnessed in the companion documentary *The American Dreamer* (1971), which will be discussed later in this chapter.

The film's narrative is as follows. Set in the Peruvian town of Chinchero, where a Hollywood production crew is making a generic Western, the film's protagonist Kansas (Dennis Hopper), a movie stunt coordinator and horse handler, witnesses the accidental death of an actor on set. Instead of returning to Hollywood along with the rest of the crew, he stays behind and becomes romantically involved with a local sex worker named Maria (Stella Garcia). Kansas integrates with the Peruvian villagers hoping to open the Chinchero region to future Hollywood film productions. After witnessing countless stuntmen seemingly gunned down, or falling off the tops of tavern roofs, and then getting up and dusting themselves off, the Chinchero villagers perceive some sort of black magic, or spiritual presence within the movies. The villagers begin to re-enact scenes they witnessed as a religious ritual. They construct cameras and tripods made of wood and junk in place of real film equipment. The staged violence witnessed during the film shoot becomes real violence toward the community as Kansas is captured, imprisoned, beaten, and seemingly sacrificed to the villagers' new movie gods.

Within the main narrative, small subplots exist that never truly come to fruition. These are obviously elements of Stern's original screenplay that were jettisoned in favor of experimental flourishes during the production and editing process. One example is Kansas's friend Neville (Don Gordon), who arrives in town to coerce Kansas and his wealthy American friends into purchasing a nearby gold mine. Kansas and Neville set off on horses for an expedition across rural Peru in search of the mine. But its isolated location means the two would-be gold prospectors would not make any profit on it. This subplot could have materialized as an *Easy Rider*-style searchers' journey across László Kovács's beautifully shot Peruvian landscape with the two men connecting or detaching along the way. Instead, this plot point along with Neville fades away without explanation.

The Last Movie won the CIDALC Award at the 1971 Venice Film Festival, an honor that should have translated to a much-anticipated North American release. Yet the film's original New York and Los Angeles screenings lasted only two weeks. The film also failed to gain respectable mainstream reviews from movie critics. Roger Ebert called it a "wasteland of cinematic wreckage . . . , undisciplined, incoherent, a structural mess."[4] The film is indeed all of these things, but Ebert and his cohort of American film critics potentially saw *The Last Movie*'s deconstruction of cinematic norms as an attack on the industry they cherished. Although it is hard to imagine a mainstream American audience embracing *The Last Movie*, the fact that it was never given an opportunity to be even mildly successful on the art-house or university circuit is a great shame. With the critical and commercial failure, Hopper's desire to make important, socially conscious, and culturally aware films evaporated almost overnight. For the remainder of the decade, he was persona non grata.

Despite this, *The Last Movie* is an accomplished example of artistic cinema that "has more in common with the psychedelic midnight movies of the late '60s and early '70s, than anything produced by a major Hollywood studio."[5] The film's nonlinear fragments flow on a phantasmagoria of sound and images that conjure up a disjointed yet illuminating experience. Andrew Tracy, in his critique of the film, considers that the "overall effect" and subject of the film "is to remove the viewer from any kind of perspectival perch, to erase the illusion of a guiding viewpoint and a stable base of judgment and force the viewer to confront the film as a persistently confounding object." Tracy continues that Hopper's "method, in both cutting and composition, is to effect a flattening of perspective within the frame, to run his varying realities together simultaneously."[6] This critique points out that the way to understand *The Last Movie* as a cinematic experience is to disconnect from the perceived narrative and observe the film like one might observe a painting or sculptural object in an art gallery. From this perspective, the film begins to make sense and becomes an immersive and, one might add, entertaining experience.

Hopper noted that the destabilizing effect of the film was purposeful:

I'm constantly reminding you that we're making a movie. I'm constantly making references to the fact that maybe you're just being silly sitting in an audience, being sucked into a movie, and starting to believe it – and then I jar you out of it.[7]

Hopper performs this "jarring" effect throughout with the inclusion of "scene missing" cards that flash up and the churn of camera reels turning within the film's sound. As Barbara Scharres notes, Hopper "destroys our naivete by destroying the illusion we have paid for."[8] With this in mind, it seems that Hopper's intention was to create an artistic audio-visual object as opposed to a traditional film.

Another way to view *The Last Movie* is as an ethnography – a way in which one can study a culture and people by complete immersion into it, or in this film's case, by exploitation of that culture. But this ethnography has now expanded to include not just a survey of the Hollywood interpretation of Chinchero indigenous culture present within the film. In retrospect, it is an immersive look at filmmaking and the New Hollywood culture of the late 1960s and early 1970s. For the audience, the death of the 1960s counterculture can be witnessed, not just on screen but in the surrounding environment of the film's production. The film is a meditation "on colonialist desire, and by extension" it becomes a "proto-treatise on white liberal guilt."[9] This perspective is taken by Scharres, who states that the audience of the film is implicated in this immersion/exploitation: "Kansas is guilty of participation in the moviemaking process, which exploits the Peruvian culture and land and introduces strange ways and discontent into the lives of the Indians."[10] Scharres goes on to say that "Hopper's disruption of the narrative with scenes of moviemaking apparatus are a jarring reminder that this same exploitation is actually taking place, perpetrated by Hopper the director; moreover, it is being done for our entertainment."[11] Hopper makes the audience implicit in the notion that movies can be exploitative from both the production and the consumption of them. Hopper's desire was to make film and art an immersive and sensory experience that would force the audience to think and feel. This immersion is aided further by the film's soundtrack.

Hopper approaches the soundtrack of *The Last Movie* differently to the music compilation style of *Easy Rider*. Rather than selecting songs directly from popular bands' or artists' studio albums and compiling a soundtrack, *The Last Movie*'s soundtrack comes direct from on-set sound recordings featured within the film itself. Jessica Hundley, part of the team responsible for restoring and

Figure 2.1 Sometimes *The Last Movie*'s visuals and soundtrack converge to create a genuine visual beauty. Here Kansas (Dennis Hopper) and Marie (Stella Garcia) kiss in a meadow with only the sound of the wind.
Source: *The Last Movie*

releasing *The Last Movie* soundtrack in 2020, wrote that "every song included was recorded originally on the set of the film, and the result is an immediate sonic intimacy"; the soundtrack recording "ultimately follows the film's own narrative arc."[12] Unlike the pristine studio recordings of the *Easy Rider* soundtrack, here recordings are rough, drenched in microphone hiss, overlapping sound and conversations, and with abrupt stoppages that follow the film's editorial cuts.

The base soundtrack of *The Last Movie* is an intermixed mosaic of Peruvian indigenous music, violins, flutes, bells, whistles, drums, horns, and groups of singing children. Live recordings of songs and background sound blend to create a "weird, experimental, abstract sonic document"[13] that meshes and pulls the audience into the film's "sonic intimacy" that Hundley described above. The combined sound and visuals envelop the audience, creating an immersive audio-visual experience. Sometimes the sound, as from the opening scene, bleeds into the music creating an overwhelming sense of volume and disorientation. With the quick-cut visual editing style and the use of overlapping sound, we are thrown into the same style of fast-paced editing witnessed in the trip scene from *Easy Rider*. This call-back to Hopper's previous film will not be the last. Later in *The Last Movie*, the loud thundering machine that provided the steady "beat" within the trip scene returns to haunt the film's last moments.

The chaotic sound and visuals of *The Last Movie*'s opening scene abruptly cut to the folky acoustic guitar strums of "Me and Bobby McGee," sung on this occasion by the song's original composer Kris Kristofferson, as Kansas rides around the mountainous pastoral landscape of Chinchero. This abrupt cut in

Figure 2.2 Much like the "acid trip" in *Easy Rider*, the overlapping "in film" audio in *The Last Movie* is designed to be destabilizing and disjointed.
Source: *The Last Movie*

visuals and sound is a staple of *The Last Movie*'s style. Hopper does not seem to want to let the audience become accustomed to what might be perceived as a typical cinematic experience. He is looking to destabilize the viewer with editorial cuts, overlapping diegetic sound, and moments that pull away from the film's narrative with "filmmaking devices such as rough jump-edits, production sequences, . . . and the sound of rolling film reels [that] blend into the background chatter."[14]

Hopper uses sound-cutting and blending to great effect during a scene in which the American film crew is partying in celebration of wrapping up the film shoot and readying to return to Hollywood. Kansas stands to one side as a group of musicians (John Buck Wilkins, Michelle Phillips, and Kris Kristofferson) harmonizes a song on acoustic guitars. Kansas exits the room and wanders into the next, which is occupied by a group of party attendees dancing around to an out-of-tune piano. Kansas continues through the house and encounters yet another group of stoned people listening to a repeated chant of "Inca" and a chiming fingerbell. The song from the first room then drifts back into the soundtrack as Kansas breaks down in tears. This scene, and its sonic component, is deeply affecting. With its use of overlapping and differing music styles, it conjures up the chaos of the party but also the overwhelming waves of emotion that Kansas is experiencing. As the sounds from each room blend, the scene becomes unbearable, and Kansas breaks down into tears, which seems an appropriate response to such overwhelming stimulation. The scene is also affecting because, as Matthieu Orlean points out, "we know very little about the character at this stage. It's as if the viewer is suddenly pierced by a very brutal, frontal emotion."[15] Without exposition or dialogue, the audio lets us know Kansas's fragile emotional state.

Kristofferson's "Me and Bobby McGee" is a song that makes regular appearances throughout the film, and at the time of the film's production the version presented here was the first airing of the song. It would appear on Kristofferson's self-titled 1970 debut record, yet the song would not reach prominence until covered by Janis Joplin and released posthumously in 1971. While Kansas is out riding his horse, Kristofferson and Phillips perform a harmonized rendition of "Me and Bobby McGee" on a nearby mountainside, which is then interrupted by Kristofferson motioning to a passing Kansas that the film crew is out looking for him.

It is worth offering a comparison of *The Last Movie* to L.M. Kit Carson's and Lawrence Schiller's documentary companion piece *The American Dreamer* (1971). While not directed by Hopper, it becomes abundantly clear during the documentary that Hopper guided the filmmakers and the subject matter to his desire. The focus on the intensive, and self-destructive, post-production process of *The Last Movie* serves as a "documentary and part fiction, part natural and part scripted"[16] representation of Hopper as an outlaw of the counterculture. Hopper interacts with the documentarians as they film. Much like a director would, he offers instructions and advice about lighting techniques and shooting locations. To camera, Hopper, self-aggrandizing, proclaims the documentary to be "a witness to myself."

The documentary gives Hopper ample room to speculate on life, politics, his childhood, the nature of film and art, religion, and sex. These stream-of-consciousness mutterings bear resemblance to the off-kilter statements and jittery persona of Hopper's photojournalist character in *Apocalypse Now* (1976). Like that character, Hopper has too many thoughts entering his head at the same time, and the only way to clear them is to blurt them out at a rapid-fire speed.

The American Dreamer adds to the mythical crazed gun-toting artistic genius that Hopper was attempting to establish around himself. The rambling interviews interspersed with footage of Hopper – bearded and in ragged jeans, gun held under arm, walking over windswept landscapes, accompanied by rough and rambling folk songs by Nashville session musician John Buck Wilkin – are partly evocative, at least from the Hollywood interpretation, of the outlaws and bandits that roamed the frontier wilderness of early America.

The documentary demonstrates the many distractions and temptations that Hopper faced in the aftermath of *Easy Rider*'s success. Drugs, drink, and fan adoration pull him away from the task of editing *The Last Movie*. And it is made clear by the constant yawning and bored expressions that Hopper had little interest in the initial stages of editing the forty-eight hours of footage shot in Peru. He only becomes interested when the images begin to take shape, and a vision of the film materializes.

One scene that illustrates this level of distraction is when a group of girls (presumably Playboy Bunnies, as this is a recurrent theme of Hopper's fantasies that he divulges to camera) are driven out to his Taos compound to actively participate in group sex, or a "sensitivity encounter," as Hopper describes it. With his manic stare, shaggy beard, and long hair, Hopper resembles cult leader Charles Manson. And the rambling and live-recorded folk music of John Buck Wilkin that populates the soundtrack of *The American Dreamer* bears similarities to Manson's own excursions into folk music before he became a notorious cult leader.

The soundtrack that accompanies the documentary is a collection of majestic Bob Dylanesque folk compositions inspired by Hopper's jaunt to Peru. The songs are fed through the filter of Hopper's persona either with some direct lyrical reference or just by sheer coincidence. A song such as "Screaming Metaphysical Blues," written and performed by John Buck Wilkin, makes direct reference to Hopper's Peruvian trip and acknowledges that the film was funded by greedy studio bosses who now want to market the counterculture right back to itself. The lyrics included within "Screaming Metaphysical Blues" that refer to finding "freedom" echo the sentiment of Dylan's use of being "free" from "The Ballad of Easy Rider." Only in death will freedom be found.

Wilkin supplies the audio bridge from *The Last Movie* to *The American Dreamer*. His compositions appear on both soundtracks, and he sums up both the destabilizing film Hopper produced and the confused reaction from Universal Pictures when they were not handed another *Easy Rider*.

Lew Wasserman, an executive of Universal, informed Hopper: "Art is only worth something if you're dead. We'll only make money on this picture if you die."[17] Hopper's death was only metaphorical. His expulsion from Hollywood and his second exile to the wilderness of American indie and foreign film for the remainder of the 1970s and early 1980s for the perceived disaster of *The Last Movie* was his actual fate.

Chris Sikelianos' contribution to the documentary's soundtrack, "Easy Rider, 1970," is a ramshackle live recording in a room where Hopper and his cohort make jokes, laugh, and talk in the background of the recording. The two songs by Byrds founding member Gene Clark – "The American Dreamer" and "Outlaw Song" – are about Hopper's desire to take a "stand," push his "boundaries," and be an "extremer."

The American Dreamer soundtrack is a hybrid of *Easy Rider* and *The Last Movie*'s soundtracking styles. Live recorded musical compositions play over montages of Hopper driving across landscapes similar to those traversed by Billy and Wyatt. Yet these recorded compositions are cut into by overlapping diegetic sounds of indigenous music (the location of *The American Dreamer* is predominantly rural Taos, New Mexico), church bells, gunshots, film reels turning and the rumble of film cutting machines, and scattered conversations, and in this respect the soundtrack resembles that of *The Last Movie*.

I would argue that the soundtrack for *The Last Movie* is the most successful use of *sound* in any of Hopper's directorial films. Hopper does not rely on popular songs; instead, he intercuts snippets of familiar Western-style folk music with indigenous music, diegetic sounds, voices, the whirl of camera films, and horses' hoofs clomping on the dirt to create an audio collage that immerses the viewer into the film. The sonic maw created by *The Last Movie* prompts the audience into a state of overwhelming dread; it also, as Carol Becker notes in her introduction to *The Subversive Imagination: The Artist, Society and Social Responsibility*, offers "a challenging source of pleasure."[18]

In an interview on *The Merv Griffin Show* in 1971, which was conducted during the critical backlash of *The Last Movie*, a disgruntled, though somewhat apologetic Hopper explained that he planned to simplify his future directorial work, "so that people can understand it and follow it as they did in *Easy Rider*." His intention, he explained, was to "become a social critic, again."[19] It is interesting that Hopper believed that simplifying his work was the way to become a social critic. The responsibility of the socially conscious artist, according to Becker, should focus "directly on the issues of daily life," and "to reveal contradictions and not obfuscate them."[20] *The Last Movie* performs this task.

Hopper did not follow through on his promise – at least, not in the foreseeable future. His last three films are certainly simpler and romanticized, with the social commentary mostly absent. But *The Last Movie* appears to be "deliberately difficult" and so the audience reaction to it was, as Becker notes, "rage and confrontation."[21] *The American Dreamer*, and to some extent, Hopper's appearance on *The Merv Griffin Show* positions Hopper as a hard-done-by artist who to his mind became "unappreciated and . . . misunderstood."[22] For the artists, the outcome of these circumstances is "rebellion (either through form or content) as a method of retaliation."[23] This is certainly the condition of Hopper's subsequent film work as an actor and, as discussed in the following chapter, his next directorial film.

Notes

1 Albert Auster and Leonard Quart, *American Film and Society Since 1945* (Santa Barbara: Praeger, 2011), 98.
2 Eric Kohn, "The Last Movie: Dennis Hopper's Misunderstood Masterpiece Deserves a Second Chance – and Now, It's Getting One," *Indiewire*, 2 August 2019 (available at www.indiewire.com/2018/08/the-last-movie-dennis-hopper-restoration-1201990114/).
3 Margy Rochlin, "Stewart Stern Out of the Soul," in *Backstory 2: Interviews with Screenwriters of the 1940s and 1950s*, ed. Pat McGilligan (Los Angeles: University of California Press, 1997), 304.
4 Roger Ebert, "The Last Movie/Chincero Movie Review," *Rogerebert.Com*, January 1971 (available at www.rogerebert.com/reviews/the-last-movie – chinchero-1971).
5 Kohn, "The Last Movie."
6 Andrew Tracy, "(En)fin de cinema *The Last Movie*," *Reverse Shot*, 4 October 2004 (available at www.reverseshot.org/symposiums/entry/235/last_movie).
7 James King, "The Punishment Remains the Same – Reflecting on Dennis Hopper's *The Last Movie*," *HOME*, 12 December 2018 (available at https://homemcr.org/article/the-punishment-remains-the-same-reflecting-on-dennis-hoppers-the-last-movie/).

8 Barbara Scharres, "From Out of the Blue: The Return of Dennis Hopper," *Journal of the University Film and Video Association* 35, no. 2, Spring 1983 (available at www.jstor.org/stable/20686939).
9 Kohn, "The Last Movie."
10 Scharres, "From Out of the Blue."
11 Ibid.
12 Jessica Hundley and Pat Thomas, "Dennis Hopper's Legendary 'Last Movie' Finally Gets a Soundtrack Album, Five Decades Later, Via Record Store Day," *Variety*, 28 August 2020 (available at https://variety.com/2020/music/news/last-movie-soundtrack-record-store-day-vinyl-exclusive-dennis-hopper-1234752570/).
13 Ibid.
14 Jefferson Patrey, "Dennis Hopper's "The Last Movie" at Northwest Film Forum," *Adventures in Sight and Sound Blog*, 18 August 2018 (available at https://blog.adventuresinsightandsound.com/2018/08/dennis-hoppers-last-movie-at-northwest.html).
15 Matthieu Orlean, "Photography, Writing, Acting . . . Movie-Making had Everything in One Package: Interview with Dennis Hopper," in *Dennis Hopper and the New Hollywood* (Paris: Flammarion, 2009), 132.
16 Unknown author, "American Dreamer: A Look at Dennis Hopper," *Ransom Note*, 19 August 2021 (available at www.theransomnote.com/art-culture/reviews-art-culture/american-dreamer-a-look-at-dennis-hopper/).
17 Peter M. Brant and Tony Shafrazi, "Dennis Hopper Part Two," *Interview Magazine*, 6 August 2010 (available at www.interviewmagazine.com/film/dennis-hopper-part-two).
18 Carol Becker, *The Subversive Imagination: Artists, Society & Social Responsibility* (New York: Routledge, 1994), xiv.
19 Hopper appeared on Season One, Episode 15 of *The Merv Griffin Show* (1971). The episode can be found at https://tubitv.com/tv-shows/501200/s01-e15-episode-15.
20 Becker, *The Subversive Imagination*, xiii.
21 Ibid.
22 Ibid.
23 Ibid.

3 Kill All Hippies

Punk Rock Rebellion, Elvis Presley, and Generational "Burn Out" in *Out of the Blue*

Dennis Hopper's third directorial film, *Out of the Blue* (1980), came midway through Hopper's exile from mainstream American cinema and culture. The critical and commercial failure of *The Last Movie* was a factor in his expulsion. The funding and responsibility placed on Hopper to develop *Easy Rider*-style cinematic milestones had not paid off and the flux of New Hollywood films that came after *Easy Rider* and *The Last Movie* dried up with the return of "event" movie blockbusters such as Steven Spielberg's *Jaws* (1975) and George Lucas's *Star Wars* (1977). Yet Hopper's 1970s period is perhaps one of his most intriguing in terms of the acting roles he was offered. Unable to secure lead performances in mainstream films, Hopper appeared in independent films such as James Frawley's comedy western *Kid Blue* (1973) and Henry Jaglom's Vietnam drama *Tracks* (1976). His appearance as Australian bushranger Daniel Morgan in Philippe Mora's *Mad Dog Morgan* (1976) was notable for the crazed performance and questionable Irish accent Hopper adopted. Yet the relative restraint he showed in Wim Wenders's *The American Friend* (1977) as suave, yet troubled art dealer Tom Ripley was revelatory, and emphasized what a fine actor he could be. However, the obscure trifecta of European films at the decade's end – *Couleur Chair* (1978), *L'Ordre et la sécurité du monde* (1978), and *Las Flores Del Vicio* (1979) – demonstrated that Hopper was as far away from Hollywood and American cinema as he could get. While this period offered only a handful of films, the performances are a fascinating insight into an actor in freefall.

Hopper's return to North American cinema was not for a Hollywood epic or a low-budget American indie film but for a Canadian television production titled *The Case of Cindy Barnes*. Hopper was cast in a supporting role as a father to a troubled teenage girl who experiences neglect and abuse. The production's original director and screenwriter Leonard Yakir abandoned the shoot after a few weeks of filming turned up no usable footage. The production was all but abandoned until Hopper saw an opportunity to take over the film. He convinced the financial backers to give him a shot at directing the film. With little to lose, they agreed, if Hopper could complete it on time and within budget.

DOI: 10.4324/9781003465843-4

Feeling the film was a potential lost cause anyway, they gave Hopper creative control and allowed him to rewrite the screenplay.

Hopper's vision was far more pessimistic and nihilistic and now dealt with teen rebel Cebe (Linda Manz) and her misfit family. Although headstrong and independent, Cebe harbors an infatuation with doomed male icons such as Elvis Presley and Syd Vicious and a love of punk rock. As a child, Cebe suffered abuse at the hands of her alcoholic father Don (Hopper) who has been imprisoned for several years after crashing his truck into a stalled school bus while drinking and being distracted by a young Cebe who was in the passenger seat. The incident killed and injured a group of school children, and the community is still baying for vengeance. Facing release, Don's intention is to restart his family life with Cebe and her mother Kathy (Sharon Farrell). Don's attempts at normal family life, however, are warped. He turns up with a can of beer to pick up Cebe from school; he makes Kathy ditch her job in a restaurant and takes her and Cebe on a picnic to a freezing cold beach and gets angry when Kathy complains. The demons that lurk in Don's subconscious rear their ugly heads once again, and he descends into a spiral of drink, drugs, and self-destruction.

In his multifaceted role as director, screenwriter, and actor, Hopper reduced, replaced, and expanded several key characters within the film. Raymond Burr's psychiatrist character, for example, was originally to have been a leading figure, but his role was reduced to a cameo in the finished film (although Burr was given enough screen time to secure the film's status as a Canadian tax-shelter production).

The typical on-site dramas of a Dennis Hopper production followed with Sharon Farrell referring to Hopper as "our director, our writer, and our dealer."[1] Despite this, *Out of the Blue* remains a straightforward, steady, and coherent film that contains some exceptional performances from its cast. Farrell's portrayal of Kathy is a case in point. She carries the weight of parental regret and shame. Her own drug dependency and inability to protect herself and her daughter from Don's abuse hangs around her neck like a cursed chalice. Linda Manz's performance as the young Cebe is extraordinary. Tough and streetwise beyond her years, she carries herself like a swaggering punk savage. Of course, this toughness comes from burying years of abuse, and, in the absence of her father, Cebe also has become the male-like figure of her household and keeps her mom's behavior in check. Hopper's protagonists from his previous films seem to drift into destruction that they never see approaching, a kind of "idealized freedom" where they "romanticized themselves and then destroyed themselves in ironic completion of denial of romantic myth"; they "are strangely blind to, the one thing we know with absolute certainty will pull the rug out from under their feet."[2] Cebe is different from other Hopper-directed protagonists, because "she will deliberately choose her destruction rather than suffer it."[3] Like the punk slogan she repeatedly uses, she "subverts normality." She knows that destruction is just around the corner and that everybody in her life is on a death trip. She embraces it. For all the strength Hopper supposedly places in his male protagonists, it is somewhat ironic that the only female lead he directed is as tough as nails.

Hopper's performance as Don is also something to consider. He is deeply troubled, regretful of his past yet unable to reconcile with the community nor with his family for the devastation he caused. His destructive tendencies float to the surface in small outbursts of anger and frustration that boil up to all-out violence. Hopper stated that he viewed *Out of the Blue* as a "spiritual and stylistic"[4] sequel to *Easy Rider*, a tale of what might have occurred had his character Billy survived the bike crash at the end of the film and rode out to some deadbeat town to marry and settle while carrying the same inadequacies that fed into Billy's circumstances. There is even a glimpse of a framed photograph of a young Don and Kathy straddling a motorcycle, like Marlon Brando in *The Wild One*, hinting that Don was once a biker and Kathy his "moll."

Out of the Blue was filmed in a short, turbulent, four-week period and edited within six weeks. It is possibly Hopper's tightest and most straightforward film, even though its themes are disturbing and complex. The film's title change reflected the repeated use of Neil Young's brooding acoustic song "My My, Hey Hey (Out of the Blue)" on the soundtrack. The song reflects the dire situation within the film, but also the changing cultural landscapes of North American society. Young's composition is the "death knell of 60s rock, in the face of punk's ascendant rancidity,"[5] when hippie burnouts like Young and Hopper were being side-lined by Syd Vicious and Johnny Rotten of the Sex Pistols and the punk rock movement in the United Kingdom and the United States that denounced the hippies.

Film critic Jonathan Rosenbaum, writing for the *Chicago Reader*, placed *Out of the Blue* in his top fifteen films of the 1980s, stating that the "bankruptcy of the parents' 1950 generation virtually metamorphosizes itself into the desperate death wish of Cebe's burnt-out 1980s mentality."[6] Hopper's generational call and response is evident. It is in the narrative of the war between the generations, in this case the Silent Generation and the Baby Boomers that followed them, and the Generation Xers. While this antagonism plays out on screen it is also there within the music contained in the soundtrack.

Out of the Blue's commercial failure at the time of its release came from the provocative subject matter of child abuse, incest, and the corrosion of the Nuclear Family. This was hardly a positive selling point to an audience wishing to embrace the conservative outlook of traditional family values and patriotic vigor that was being pushed by Ronald Reagan's presidential campaign run at the time of the film's production. It is interesting to consider that Hopper would later become a Republican voter even as he embraced the very opposite of Reagan's conservative values and was openly critical of certain policies in his artistic work. This would become an odd schism in Hopper's output as his career progressed and faced an upturn later in the decade.

Reagan's campaign slogan of "Let's Make America Great Again" was a reactionary statement to the ethos of Hopper's generation and to the often-inflammatory art they produced. It was an effort to take America back to the time before the 1960s and to nullify the progress of racial and gender equality and sexual emancipation, a movement toward what the character George Hanson in *Easy Rider* deemed to be "one helluva good country" before the 1960s turned it on its head. It was a campaign to erase the social gains of the 1960s, and it would succeed in some quarters with the "once radicalized counterculture generation" who had by now "lost their youth and with it, the change-the-world aspirations of a now mythological time all eroded through an ensuing decade of deflation and apathy, the void filled with insularity and affluence."[7]

Unable to sustain the ideals of the 1960s, the hippies and other so-called radicals adapted to America's prosperity and consolidated themselves within it. This was already in motion as the 1960s were coming to an end and can be witnessed in *Easy Rider* as Billy and Wyatt lead the charge out of the promised collective utopianism and into personal wealth that they believe will bring them personal freedom.

North America was not the place to sell *Out of the Blue*'s nihilistic point of view. Europe was more responsive to the film, although it did remain banned in the United Kingdom until 1987. The film amassed a cult following with audiences seeking it at late-night theater screenings and finding shoddy VHS copies to view at home.

Hollywood did not come crawling back apologetic with an acceptance that they had been wrong to jettison Hopper from the film industry for a second time. Hopper had succeeded in producing a film that was so disconnected from the zeitgeist that nobody in their right mind would allow his nightmarish vision on screen until it could be softened – or until there came a point in time when audiences could accept Hopper's uncompromising position. This is what has occurred with much of Hopper's work, including *Out of the Blue*. As *Out of the Blue* approached its fortieth anniversary, a Kickstarter campaign organized by the film's producers John Alan Simon and Elizabeth Karr of Discovery Pictures exceeded its target and enabled them to restore the film to a 4K digital print, to release the film into select movie theaters and film festivals worldwide, and to issue it on DVD and Blu-ray. The film's high-profile champions, including actress Chloë Sevigny and filmmaker Richard Linklater, positioned it for new audiences to discover. As occurred with Hopper's *The Last Movie* and its re-evaluation and reissue, the decades and the changes in society have rendered *Out of the Blue* an essential artifact of cultural importance.

One aspect of the film that enables *Out of the Blue* to sustain interest is its association with the punk rock movement. This association exists despite very little punk rock being included on the soundtrack. There is a look and feel to the film that evokes the danger and provocation of punk's defiant attitude toward everything. It is there in Cebe's confrontational slogans, like "Disco sucks!"

Figure 3.1 Although seemingly untrained Cebe has ambition to be a punk rock star.
Source: *Out of the Blue*

and "Punk is not sexual it's just aggression," that she bellows to random truckers on the CB radio in Don's abandoned truck. The grimy quality of the film (before the restoration, that is) as it jumped from a damaged film reel to countless VHS cassettes means that many people first saw this film in some state of degradation.

Alongside an original score provided by record producer and composer Tom Lavin, the music Hopper additionally chose to soundtrack *Out of the Blue* summons a wide array of emotions that encounter the loss of childhood innocence and the gloom that follows. It also bridges the generational gaps of the 1950s, the 1960s, and the late 1970s by incorporating music from all these eras and demonstrating a rough evolution of popular music for these generations.

This begins with Elvis Presley's upbeat "My Teddy Bear" heard on the soundtrack and sung by a young Cebe to Don as it blasts from his truck radio. Cebe idolizes Presley and is troubled by his death. She wears an Elvis-emblazoned studded denim jacket and refers to him as "the first punk." Cebe informs Kathy that "Elvis died on me so I'm gonna kill myself so I can go visit him." For many who grew up with "The King," his death in 1977 was a generational loss.

When we meet with Cebe five years after the accident, "My Teddy Bear" has been replaced by Presley's more somber "Heartbreak Hotel." Cebe listens to the song on her portable tape player and sings along to the downbeat lyrics of lost love. In this context, the song offers some strange hope that the return of Don will end her loneliness and make her and her mother happy once again.

We also see Cebe's bedroom adorned with posters of punk rockers and a shrine to Presley. In her room is a set of drums that she bangs aimlessly on and a guitar that she cannot play but places close to the amplifier to create a sonic wall of distortion. She has ambitions to be a famous punk rock star.

Neil Young's brooding "My My, Hey Hey (Out of the Blue)" is the film's recurring signature song which evokes images of "burning out" and "fading away." This echoes the nihilistic ending of the film in which Cebe murders Don by stabbing him, and then proceeds to kill herself and Kathy by blowing up Don's derelict truck with dynamite while they are locked together in the cab. Cebe literally and brightly burns out and maintains the tradition of Hopper's films ending in fire. Young also sings about passing the mantle from one generation to another, in this case, from Elvis Presley to Johnny Rotten and the punk rock generation.

Hopper captures the impression of impending doom that lies at the heart of Young's composition. An act a decade and half later on from *Out of the Blue* would capture it further for another generation when Kurt Cobain, lead singer and guitarist with grunge rock band Nirvana, committed suicide on 5 April 1994, at the age of 27. Nirvana had become a sensation; a very bright and short burst of punk-infused energy propelled them to international stardom and Cobain to somewhat unwanted adoration. Songs such as "Smells Like Teen Spirit," "Come as You Are," and "Heart Shaped Box," among others, became anthems for bored, and disenfranchised youth. When Cebe talks about her heroes Johnny Rotten, Syd Vicious, and Elvis Presley, she could have also been talking about Cobain. Cebe's brand of rebellion and teenage alienation, one attached to infatuation of singular male figures, would have embraced the enigmatic Cobain in the late 1980s when the band appeared on Sub-Pop records with the debut album *Bleach*. When Cobain's body was discovered, the suicide note that lay beside his body drew much speculation. The most notable aspect was Cobain's use of Young's lyrics from "My My, Hey Hey (Out of the Blue)" as a final sign-off. Cobain, like Cebe in *Out of the Blue*, chose to "burn out" rather than fade away. Cebe's was a literal, and small-town interpretation of Young's lyrics; Cobain's actions, like Presley's death, rocked an entire generation.[8]

Hopper uses lyrical call-backs from "My My, Hey Hey (Out of the Blue)" within the dialogue for emphasis. In *Out of the Blue*, Cebe enters a diner and gets hassled by a girl who accuses her father of being responsible for the death of her little brother in the bus crash. As the argument escalates, Cebe retaliates by smearing a blue ice cream cone over the girl's face and proclaiming: "I've painted your face blue, it looks better that way, and if you don't shut up and get outta here I'm gonna take you out of the blue and put you into the black." Cebe then hits a button on her portable tape player and the first chords of "My My, Hey Hey (Out of the Blue)" are broadcast from the speakers as she storms out.

Out of the Blue also incorporates live performances into the narrative. After seeing her mother shooting up with Don's best friend Charlie (Don Gordon playing another lousy associate to Hopper's character), she runs away and hitches a ride into the city. Cebe wanders downtown. She stumbles into a street performer wearing a tight-fitting Presley-style jumpsuit and singing a mutant rendition of Presley's song "Are You Lonesome Tonight?" In comparison to the destabilizing effect Hopper deployed in *The Last Movie*, the audience is jettisoned out of the film's narrative for a moment as the performer turns to the camera and asks if the shot was okay. The cast and crew (including an audible Hopper) cheer and clap in delight. Cebe's night takes a sinister turn when she accepts an invitation from a cab driver to go smoke pot and party at his place. When he attempts to rape her, she smashes his head with a lamp and makes a run for it.

She then stumbles into Vancouver's Viking Hall and encounters Canadian punk band The Pointed Sticks performing live to a raucous crowd. She is invited by Sticks drummer Ian Tiles to bash at the skins as the band rattles through a rendition of their songs "Out of Luck" and "Somebody's Mom." Oddly enough, the version of "Out of Luck" is a studio-recorded version that the band mimes along to, while "Somebody's Mom" is taken directly from the concert's recorded sound. The whole performance is chaotic and captures the raw energy of the punk movement.

This scene is the one act of catharsis within the film. Cebe is allowed to enjoy this moment. Her involvement in the music and the praise she receives from the crew backstage offer a brief insight into what could have been. Another life is waiting for her away from the familial destruction and her small-minded town. With her entourage in tow, Cebe gets behind the wheel of a car. She experiences a flashback to the crash that killed the school kids and sent her dad to jail. She makes the same mistake her father made and crashes the car. And this begins Cebe's downward spiral.

Hopper must have an affinity for the chaotic and improvisational energy of live performances as they are included in many of his films. *Easy Rider* featured street performances during the New Orleans Mardi Gras scenes, and *The Last*

Figure 3.2 While wandering the streets of Vancouver, Cebe encounters a street crooner singing an Elvis Presley song.

Source: *Out of the Blue*

Movie's soundtrack was all on-set live recordings of singers performing. Here we are treated to a filmed concert that moves with the speed and visual flare of an MTV-style music video. According to Pointed Sticks lead singer Nick Jones, Hopper created an atmosphere of tension within the performance; he said that Hopper "never showed up until after midnight with his camera crew, so people have been there for twelve hours in this place, so you can imagine how tense the whole thing was at that point: kids were drunk, passed out."[9] What Hopper captures on film is the orgasmic explosion of that tension releasing.

Despite *Easy Rider* laying the foundations of the music-video format and the scenes of live performance on display in *Out of the Blue*, Hopper never chose to direct music videos or, like some of his fellow directors, film live concerts by the innumerable musicians and bands he associated with or by the punks, new romantics, and grunge rockers of the late 1980s and early 1990s. His visual flare, fast-paced editing, use of metaphor and emphasis, plus his leanings toward on-set drama, would have proved vital for such an engagement and would have flipped the usual progression of film directors such as Spike Jones and Michel Gondry starting their careers in music video and commercials and progressing on to feature films. Hopper certainly enjoyed playing roles in music-centric films. His harrowing portrayal as music mogul Kenneth Barlow in Roland Klick's *White Star* (1983) pulls on the eccentricity and megalomania of music stardom, although set in the squalid clubs of West Berlin. Hopper played a music-video director in Julian Temple's Mick Jagger vehicle *Running Out of Luck* (1985). Years later, Hopper would go on to lead the cast of the television show *Crash* (2008–2009) as obnoxious and maniacal Los Angeles-based music producer Ben Cendars.

The triumph of *Out of the Blue*'s soundtrack is not the content of the music as such but the trajectory that takes music of the 1950s and 1960s – the music of Don and Kathy's generation, which we witness mostly as background in the rundown honky-tonk bars that Don and his buddies frequent – and the ideals of that era that have soured toward Generation X's punk reaction to those failed ideals. The inclusion of Young's music acts as a bridge to these two conflicting music styles and sets of ideals. Young was well entrenched within the 1960s music scene as a member of the group Buffalo Springfield, as a solo artist, and as a founding member of the supergroup Crosby, Stills, Nash, and Young. Young's evolution as an artist with his band Crazy Horse on the 1979 album *Rust Never Sleeps* garnered respect from the punks, and although he remained mostly irrelevant throughout the 1980s, his return to prominence with his 1989 record *Freedom* saw his sound embraced by the post-punk and emerging grunge audiences, culminating with Young's collaboration with grunge rock superstars Pearl Jam on the 1995 album *Mirror Ball*.

The countercultural ethos that had originated in the 1960s, that of Hopper and Young, had morphed into a critical backlash of the late 1970s. Punk by its very definition was anti-authoritarian, anti-consumerism, and anti-hippy. The hippies' flowing long hair, flared pants, flowery shirts, and peaceful disposition had mutated into short spiky hair, tight bondage pants, pins, studs, and aggressive and confrontational mannerisms. The audience of Hopper's *Easy Rider*, who had embraced the ethos of peace, love, and understanding, were now in the firing line of punk rock's nihilism, and Hopper was the one holding the gun to the head of his own generation's perceived inadequacy.

Hopper's anger is channeled through Cebe. She becomes the film's anchor, hating on everyone and everything, and by the end of her short and violent journey we, the audience, feel that her actions to "burn out" are completely justified, especially after continuously hearing from Young that this is better than "fading away." Cebe snuffs out not only herself but the entire misguided judgment of the previous generation that promoted peace and equality yet sold it out. *Out of the Blue* is one long "fuck off" to the past, present, and future, which as Cebe, echoing the Sex Pistols, states are "Pretty vacant, eh?" Certainly, the mainstream culture surrounding the film might have been vacant.

Several scenes use music to convey emotion. When Don is informed that he is being fired from his landfill job he drives his excavator into the foreman's cabin and then cracks open a hip flask and takes a swig as a toast to his self-destruction. Over the scene of this carnage plays the Springsteen-esque piano and guitar of the song "Sorry Just Won't Do" by singer Jim Byrnes. Whereas "My My, Hey Hey" gives Cebe a voice and a means of expression, "Sorry Just Won't Do" gives a voice to Don's realization that his past is too complicated and too disturbing for any retribution. There is no apology that Don can muster to make amends with the community or his devastated family. Sorry, in this case, just will not cut it.

An earlier scene in the film in which Don first emerges from prison also reflects this. A party held at his home is populated by friends and acquaintances from his past. Some embrace him, others remain at a distance, and Don senses this. The tragedy shook the community, and some cannot forgive and forget. This scene is reminiscent of the moment in *The Last Movie* in which Kansas navigates through a party that is ever-changing. Don wanders through the scene in a comparable way. His emotions shift. The music and sounds change as Don moves through the small rooms. A record is playing, a partygoer with an acoustic guitar (the aforementioned Jim Byrnes) begins playing a song. The dialogue of Kathy and Don greeting people intermingle with that of the gathered group of friends as they toast Don's arrival. It is a tense scene, made more so by the conflicting music and overlapping dialogues. The scene ends abruptly when Don is confronted by a father of one of the victims of the accident. Don, in an act of intimidation and self-pity, pours a bottle of whiskey over his head and offers to take the aggressor outside to "bust some heads."

A complaint that can often be aimed at Hopper's soundtracks is the overall maleness of the compositions. Even with a female protagonist, a rarity in Hopper's films, although as witnessed in *Backtrack* and *The Hot Spot* not unheard of, the reliance is on male voices within the soundtrack. In this case, there is some reasonable justification. Cebe idolizes male rock icons like Elvis Presley, Johnny Rotten, and Syd Vicious. Their attitude and recklessness appeal to her because the only other males in her life, her father Don and his lecherous friends, are also reckless and insolent. In Cebe's mind, Don's time spent in prison gives him the same notoriety as Presley gained by shaking and thrusting his hips on live television, or that Johnny Rotten earned by snarling and cussing during a daytime interview. Cebe longs to become just like Don, or at least her idealized version of him. When she and Cathy talk about which parent she most resembles, Kathy remarks that Cebe is like Don in looks and attitude. "A girl Don," Cebe gleefully remarks. Despite their gender differences, Neil Young, Elvis Presley, and the punks of The Pointed Sticks are speaking to and for Cebe's experiences.

Despite the film being dismissed at the time by audiences, *Out of the Blue* has reverberated around the culture and elements of the film have cropped up in unexpected places. As previously mentioned, Kurt Cobain's suicide note featured a line from Neil Young's titular song. Filmmaker and artist Miranda July performed in a punk band called the CeBe Barnes Band. In 2000, the Scottish indie band Primal Scream launched their sixth album, *XTRMNTR*, with the song "Kill All Hippies," which takes its title from Cebe's popular slogan, and in its introduction the song features a sample of Cebe's monologue proclaiming "Subvert normality. Fuck you! Punk is not sexual, it's just aggression."

Notes

1 David Stewart, "Dennis Hopper's Blue Period: The Making of *Out of the Blue*," *Please Kill Me*, 4 May 2020 (available at https://pleasekillme.com/dennis-hopper-out-of-the-blue-1980/).
2 Barbara Scharres, "From Out of the Blue: The Return of Dennis Hopper,'" *Journal of the University Film and Video Association* 35, no. 2, Spring 1983 (available at www.jstor.org/stable/20686939).
3 Ibid.
4 Ben Sachs, "Dennis Hopper's *Out of the Blue* Remains a Powerful Depiction of Teen Delinquency," *Chicago Reader*, 20 September 2015 (available at https://chicagoreader.com/blogs/dennis-hoppers-out-of-the-blue-remains-a-powerful-depiction-of-teen-delinquency/).
5 Dorothy Woodend, "Out of the Blue," *The Tyee*, 12 November 2010 (available at https://thetyee.ca/ArtsAndCulture/2010/11/12/OutOfTheBlue/).
6 Jonathan Rosenbaum, "Top Ten Lists 1974–2006," *Chicago Reader via Archive.org*, 7 June 2010 (available at https://web.archive.org/web/20110607040346/http://alumnus.caltech.edu/%7Eejohnson/critics/rosenbaum.html).
7 Dean Brandum, "A Legacy Went Searching for a Film . . . Dennis Hopper and *Easy Rider*," *Senses of Cinema*, 5 April 2010 (available at www.sensesofcinema.com/2010/feature-articles/a-legacy-went-searching-for-a-film%E2%80%A6-dennis-hopper-and-easy-rider/).
8 Marco Margaritoff, "Inside the Text of Kurt Cobain's Heartwrenching Suicide Note," *All That's Interesting*, 2 January 2020 (available at https://allthatsinteresting.com/kurt-cobain-suicide-note/).
9 Stewart, "Dennis Hopper's Blue Period."

4 Rebel Without a Pause
Rap and Hip-Hop's Gang Affiliation, Popularity, and Battle with Authority in *Colors*

Out of the Blue would place Dennis Hopper out of the mainstream once again. His acting roles during the early to mid-1980s would be relegated to small parts in mostly low-budget films such as *King of the Mountain* (1981), or he would appear inebriated in films such as Neil Young's *Human Highway* (1982) and Francis Ford Coppola's *Rumble Fish* (1983). His antics would often be the center of Hopper's story more than his actual performances. During filming of *Human Highway*, for example, Hopper was throwing knives around the set (an ordinary activity for Hopper to partake in at this point) and accidentally severed a tendon in costar Sally Kirkland's finger. Kirkland would later sue Hopper, stating that he was totally out of control.[1]

Unable to score prominent acting roles in American cinema, Hopper headed to West Germany to appear as a disheveled and erratic music manager in Roland Klick's *White Star* (1984). Hopper's extremities burn through the screen; rather than offer up any direction, Klick simply points the camera at Hopper and allows him to indulge in unhinged monologues on the radicalness of the 1960s, the artistic expression, and the sex that was plentiful. *White Star* may not hang together as a coherent film, but as an experience of Hopper's dangerous and psychological decay and his character's persona bleeding into the reality of Hopper's own nature it is exhilarating to witness. *White Star* is a remarkable document of a time and place in Hopper's career when he was ejected from the mainstream, yet still immersed and dedicated to the acting performance.

The drugs and alcohol consumption eventually caught up with him on the set of Ernst Ritter von Theumer's film *Jungle Warriors* (1984). Hopper wandered off set and into the Mexico jungle after ingesting a cocktail of tequila and LSD. When the authorities tracked him down, he was naked and begging to be shot dead.[2] This episode was the catalyst for Hopper's entry into a rehabilitation program. Once he was clean and sober, Hopper would begin his journey toward a newfound respectability as an actor and a survivor of the 1960s and 1970s.

After a run of critically praised performances in David Lynch's *Blue Velvet*, Tim Hunter's *River's Edge*, and David Anspaugh's *Hoosiers* (all of which

DOI: 10.4324/9781003465843-5

appeared in 1986), Hopper was given an opportunity to return to directing with the film *Colors* (1988).

Colors features Sean Penn as rookie police officer McGavin and Robert Duvall as Hodges, a wise and seasoned officer who is paired with McGavin to show him the slow game of gang mediation and earning respectability on the street. The film also features performances from Don Cheadle and Damon Wayan as gangsters "Rocket" and "T-Bone," respectively. Cuban-born Venezuelan actress María Conchita Alonso appears as "home girl" Louisa, a love interest to McGavin. American comedian and actor Trinidad Silva appears as Leo "Frog" Lopez, the wise elder of an Hispanic street gang who has good rapport with Hodges.

In an interview with the *South Florida Sun Sentinel*, Hopper noted that the film was conceived very differently to the finished product, stating:

> It was about a white cop and a black cop in Chicago, and it involved gangs – which is where the title, *Colors*, comes from – but they were selling cough syrup. There was a major bust to stop the terrible cough syrup problem. I said, "Give me a break. Make it cocaine, make it real, make it Los Angeles. This wouldn't even make a bad episode of a television show. Why don't you make it an older cop and younger cop, make 'em white, make it about the gangs in Los Angeles.[3]

Hopper's vision for *Colors* came to pass. Real drugs and real street conflicts that were high on the news agenda at the time became the main thread of the narrative. The location of Chicago was switched to the urban sprawl of the Watts district of Los Angeles.

It might be hard to conceive of a middle-aged Hollywood player such as Hopper directing a modern (for the time, anyway) urban story of gang warfare. He pulls it off with vitality. But with the political backdrop buried and no moral stance taken, *Colors* rambles along in an atmosphere that Hal Hinson of the *Washington Post* described as "moody, dampened down" with the quagmire of "endless days spent hanging out, fried on PCP or weed" for the gang members and "days spent cruising around in the patrol car, logging in the hours, days when nothing happens"[4] for the police officers.

This criticism is fair. Certainly, events occur within the narrative of the film. There is action, tension, and a number of thrilling car chases and foot pursuits, but it is all so normalized to the point of being unremarkable for those involved. The motions of these characters' lives were set decades before, and without any massive policy intervention it continues both sides of the law. The film, in its mundanity, simply shows this endless and unchangeable process.

The sense of routine washes on the audience and a procedural weariness hovers over the film. An understanding exists between police officers, gang members, and even the audience that this situation will never resolve itself.

Perhaps the sense of "realism" that Hopper wished to portray did not quite correspond to a Hollywood action drama. This becomes more apparent when *Colors* is placed in comparison with the excitement of later "hood" films such as Spike Lee's *Do the Right Thing* (1988), John Singleton's *Boyz n the Hood* (1991), Walter Hill's *Trespass* (1992), Stephen Milburn Anderson's *South Central* (1992), and Albert and Allen Hughes's *Menace II Society* (1993). These films, it should be noted, all come from the perspective of gang members, as opposed to the police point of view that *Colors* takes.

At the time of the filming, Hopper had relocated to a Frank Gehry-designed five-parcel compound in one of the tougher neighborhoods of Venice, California. He was accustomed to witnessing the drug exchanges, shoot-ups, graffiti tagging, and fights that would occur between warring gangs. Within this atmosphere, the echoes of hip-hop and rap music could be heard drifting from the car stereos and boomboxes of passing gang members. Living in the hotbed of hip-hop and rap music's birthplace, Hopper recalled the first time he heard a rap song: "I was walking down Venice Beach, not far from my house, and I heard these guys walk by with their boomboxes. They were illegal records; this is before rap was on the radio."[5]

While "the movie's about the police, not the gangs,"[6] Hopper took the representation of gang culture seriously and scouted gang-held territory such as Watts, San Pedro, and Boyle Heights for locations and took polaroid pictures of the gang graffiti and tags that adorned walls and shopfronts and the attempts by the municipal buffing crews to cover them over. These polaroid pictures would eventually be collected in the 2017 monograph *Colors: The Polaroids* published by Damiani Editore. Hopper also cast real Crips and Bloods gang members as extras to populate scenes, explaining that "if I was shooting in a Crip area, I'd use Crips as extras. Shooting in a Blood area, I'd use Bloods."[7]

In light of the recent rise of organizations such as Black Lives Matter and the fight for racial justice and equality across the board, *Colors* has not aged well. The film's scenes of police brutality against Black gang members are distressing and uncalled for. In one scene, McGavin confiscates a spray can from a Black youth who is memorializing a deceased gang member on enemy turf and savagely sprays the kid's face before sending him on his way.

Of course, *Colors* predates the 1991 beating of Rodney King and the subsequent Los Angeles riots that took place the following year when the police officers involved in the incident were acquitted. Police brutality against Black people has continued to, and beyond, the murder of George Floyd in Minneapolis in May 2020, which set off a worldwide movement of protest and outrage against police violence. The times may have changed, but prejudice remains and demands confrontation.

With Hopper presenting the gangs from a white male perspective, it was obvious that this element of the narrative would be overlooked by many film critics at the time. Hal Hinson states that the "relationship between the two cops and the tension created by the clash of their styles is the movie's main point of interest."[8] I disagree. Both lead actors offer dynamic performances, but at no point is the audience invested in what becomes of McGavin and Hodges. The outcome is predictable. Hodges, on the brink of retirement, will die. The hothead McGavin will follow his elder's lead and become a responsible and respected officer. All this transpires.

The most interesting aspect of *Colors* is its soundtrack. The white male authoritative perspective of the film rubs up against the predominantly Black experiences and the Black-fronted music that is presented on the Warner Bros. Records soundtrack album. This music comprises contemporary hip-hop, R&B, and gangsta rap by the likes of Eric B. & Rakim, Salt-n-Pepa, MC Shan, Roxanne Shanté, and Ice-T, who supplies the film with its signature theme song "Colors." An original score is also supplied by composer and producer Herbie Hancock, and several songs by artists such as John Mellencamp, The Band, and Los Lobos appear non-diegetically within the film but are omitted from the soundtrack album. Notably, Hopper uses the folksy melody of the song "One Time One Night" by Chicano rock band Los Lobos as his opening song. Using a visual style similar to that of *Easy Rider*, Hopper uses images of the "infinite banal suburbia"[9] of the south side of Los Angeles shot from a moving vehicle as the song plays over the footage and the film's opening credits flash up. Traversing this urban landscape is reminiscent of the moment when *Easy Rider* switches gears from the folksy psychedelia of The Byrds and The Holy Modal Rollers to Jimi Hendrix's discordant guitar wails of "If 6 Were 9" while the two bikers enter the city environment, and their trip takes a darker turn.

"One Time One Night" is an interesting choice, as the song's lyrical content paints images of a fractured, violent, and pessimistic American psyche, one that is reflected in *Colors* and other Hopper-directed films. The song's lyrical concerns are reminiscent of George Hanson's casual but loaded remarks in *Easy Rider* that America "used to be one helluva good country." It appears, 19 years after *Easy Rider*'s cinematic release, that Hopper still understood the divisions and problems that most Americans endured.

The Band's inclusion in the *Colors* soundtrack is a call-back to *Easy Rider* and its use of the song "The Weight," which appeared in the film as a recorded rendition by The Band. For the *Easy Rider* soundtrack album, however, The Band's version was replaced with a performance of the song by American rock group Smith.

As mentioned, *Colors* features original music by Herbie Hancock that incorporates the beats, record scratches, and use of keyboards to form what can be considered a generic 1980s-style score. Hancock was much sought after for film scoring in 1988, coming off the back of his Oscar win for Best Original Score for Bertrand Tavernier's *Round Midnight* (1986), about the jazz scene in 1950s Paris. The win was controversial in the sense that Hancock's score had gone up against Ennio Morricone's for *The Mission* and Jerry Goldsmith's for *Hoosiers*, both original compositions in the grand tradition of film scoring. Hancock's score for *Round Midnight* consisted of well-established jazz standards by the likes of Thelonious Monk, Kenny Dorham, and Bud Powell. It was, like the soundtrack to *Easy Rider*, a compilation of prerecorded and well-known compositions. Hancock's original score for *Colors* remains unreleased on physical media at present.

The Warner soundtrack album of hip-hop and rap music reflected the lives of the gang member characters in the film. It was Hopper's update on the soundtrack style witnessed in *Easy Rider*. But there is a notable difference. Apart from the film's titular theme song, all the hip-hop tracks that appear on the Warner release feature in the film as diegetic music that plays in short bursts and lurks as part of the background sound when we see gang members talking, dancing, dealing, or hanging out. The hip-hop music is buried in the mix, creating a barely noticed soundscape that nonetheless remains incredibly important to the characters. The hip-hop and rap compositions may not take centerstage within the film's narrative, much like the gang members themselves, but they give those characters a voice and a perspective that is "told" by the track selections.

In Andrew Goodwin's book *Dancing in the Distraction Factory*, rap artist Chuck D calls hip-hop and rap music "the television of black America," a portal into the "events and environments described by the rapper."[10] Rap and hip-hop's use of sampling of the urban environment – employing gunshots, televised news reports, and police car sirens, along with the splicing, dissecting, cutting, and mixing of musical hooks from past songs – creates a soundscape that relates back to the 24/7 nature of channel flipping through cable television shows.

One of the stand-out moments of the soundtrack is MC Shan's "A Mind is a Terrible Thing to Waste." The song illustrates the reality of gang existence where members roam together as a "pack" while always looking over ones shoulder and keeping a "weapon" close while living "worried" about being "beaten." Yet Shan's rhymes articulate the negative aspect of gang life which also involves "robbin' and vickin'" and "fightin' and killin.'" Shan's statements reflect the circumstances of the film's gang members from their own perspective – that of becoming a gang affiliate for personal safety, a higher social status, and the exchange of typical familial relationships. It also takes the moral stance of the film itself that gang life does not pay off and could get you imprisoned, violently beaten, or even killed.

Urban theorist Mike Davis points this out in his forward to John Hagedorn's book *A World of Gangs: Armed Young Men and Gangsta Culture*, stating:

> Gangs, in the most straightforward sense, mint power for the otherwise powerless from their control of small urban spaces: street corners, slums, playgrounds, parks, schools, prison dormitories, even garbage dumps. For poor youth lacking other resources, these informal spatial monopolies, if successfully defended and consolidated, provide some measure of entrepreneurial opportunity as well as local prestige and warrior glamour.[11]

"A Mind is a Terrible Thing to Waste" comments on the need for gangs to exist yet is critical of the role they play in their community – a double-edged sword.

Ice-T's theme song "Colors" provides a more solid statement from the gang member perspective and forewarns the police that if they insist on removing gangs from the street it will take "work." Indeed, this work is still ongoing; gang warfare in Los Angeles is still raging, and in some areas of the city it has escalated to levels not seen since the heyday of gang violence in the mid-1980s to mid-1990s.[12] Decades of police presence and mediation have not rescinded the need for young people to turn toward gang affiliation in order to attain a social safety net that the state has revoked or barely provided in the first place.

As mentioned, the track "Colors" is heard during a scene in which gang members are rounded up by the police and briefly imprisoned in order to ease tensions on the street after a brutal shoot-up. Its non-diegetic use is jarring yet highly effective. Within the film, the song is blunt, loud, and brash, and it begs the question of why *all* the hip-hop compositions were not used as prominently as "Colors" is here.

Colors is a film that gives the impression of a faux-documentary of the Black-American and Latino gang experience of Los Angeles. Strip away the

Figure 4.1 Ice-T's theme song "Colors" intrudes upon the soundtrack when the gang members are rounded up by the cops.

Source: *Colors*

dominant police narrative, and the urban locations, hang-out spots, streets, and neighborhoods offer up an authentic look at the nature of the impoverished conditions predominantly Black and Latino people survive in. Hopper stated that the locations they shot in were places "police won't go into unless there's a body lying there."[13] The film represents a deeper problem inflicted upon urban youth by the policies of Ronald Reagan's administration and the subsequent neoliberal era that he and his government ushered in and that subsequent administrations did little to roll back on. Progress in attempting to reach racial equality, even with a sitting Black President in office between the years 2008 and 2016, has been stymied, and the policies that harm Black people and members of other disadvantaged and disenfranchised groups have continued unabated.

In 1983, the Reagan administration made severe cuts to the federal fund for employment training that was seen as a lifeline for urban youth to better themselves, to step away from their troubled neighborhoods, and to be symbols of virtue within their community. These cuts left poor and predominantly Black youth stranded and reliant on gang affiliation, drugs, theft, guns, and violence to get by. Albert Auster and Leonard Quart argue that in

> the Reagan years many of the black economic and social gains of the 1960s and 1970s, ranging from the rate of college attendance to the proportion of two-parent families to relative income levels, began to decline while poverty and crime rates escalated.[14]

Instead of forming healthy relationships with positive authority figures such as teachers, union leaders, or community organizers, young people found community ties within gang culture where the hierarchy was easier to climb and maintain than the social one, and where the rewards of respect and fear were almost instantaneous. It is interesting to see that Hopper, a Republican voter at the time of the film's production, was not blinded to the damage of some of Reagan's policies. The depiction of gang culture in *Colors* is not shaped by Hopper's political outlook at this point in his life and career. He offers a sympathetic and fair portrayal of a Los Angeles rife with conflict and division; he declines to demonize the gangs and instead portrays them as intent on survival and the protection of their fellow members.

As with much of his directorial work, Hopper could have gone further in his analysis and criticism by including rhyme and reason for the appeal of gang life. But the gangs in *Colors*, much like the police, just happen to exist. They are, as Sheila Benson notes, "rebels without a context," and Hopper does "nothing to sketch in the social and economic pressures that lead kids to see gangs as the only brotherhood in a bleak and hopeless world."[15] When questioned about what "wealthy white guys" like him and Sean Penn knew about gang culture, Hopper's answer is telling of the perspective the film takes. He stated:

> Sean got a photographer whose beat is the gang turf, and learned about it on his own. From there, we also went to O.S.S. – Operation Safe Streets, of the LA sheriff's department – and C.R.A.S.H., which Sean and Robert Duvall work for in our movie, and [which] stands for Community Resource

Figure 4.2 A majority of the hip-hop and rap music can be heard playing on stereos in the background when the gangs are hanging out.

Source: *Colors*

Against Street Hoodlums. These are the L.A.P.D. cops who go out and deal with gangs every day.[16]

The research stems from the perspective of the police officers who operate on gang territory, although Hopper, in the same interview, was clear that if the studio had not been fronting the production funds he would "probably have made it strictly about the gangs, not about the police."[17] This would have made for a more critical film, and possibly one held in higher esteem. Despite the controversy triggered by the release of *Colors*, which included boycotts and protests, and damnation from the L.A. police, it is hard to imagine those embedded within rap and hip-hop communities having much respect for the cop-loving perspective the film takes.

We must look at *Colors* through the lens of *Easy Rider*, and the culture that spawned that film, and the failures of that culture. As John Hagedorn comments in *A World of Gangs*:

> The 1960s, for a brief time, recaptured in the United States, and across the globe, a rebirth of optimism. Youth, inspired by such diverse figures as Vladimir Lenin, John Lennon, John F. Kennedy, and Bob Marley, surged to the barricades to demand that capitalism live up to its promises or relinquish power.[18]

The global radical movements that gained vital wins in equality did not go far enough for all pockets of society. Capitalism accelerated and discarded those that could not keep up. We see this malaise in *Easy Rider* as Billy and

Wyatt "drop out" of society and head off on their own tangent without a thought for the Civil Rights or anti-war movements they presumably had a hand in creating. With no follow-through from these movements of the 1960s, "the state clamped down on black, Latino, Native American, and youth rebellion, replacing the war on poverty with a war on crime, as its police gunned down and jailed Black Panthers and other radicals and rebels."[19]

As social gains stalled and were forsaken, "unsupervised peer groups, which are unsupervised because the institutions of society – schools, church, family – break down," installed their own structures within their broken communities, and "the decline of social movements . . . had the unforeseen consequence in some large cities of strengthening gangs."[20] From this emerged the rap and hip-hop music that became dominant as a form of social commentary and of recordkeeping for the Black experience, where none had existed before, on the conditions inflicted on predominantly Black communities. Rap and hip-hop also operated as music that could be used to organize makeshift block parties and to bring communities together to dance, drink, and socialize. The music evolved from the street as

> a marvelous hybrid, a merger of earlier blues, the West African griot, or call and response and emphasis on drumming, the Afro-Brazilian martial arts dance capoeira, and the Jamaican toasting tradition, as well as the African American celebration of male outlaws like "Stagger Lee." Puerto Rican and other Latino influences were present in New York in the early years, and Mexican influences helped shape West Coast rap.[21]

As rap evolved alongside gang activities and was embraced and incorporated into gang culture itself, and as that culture and lifestyle fed into the music and lyrics, it took on a harsher, more negative, and more aggressive stance that emerged as the gangsta rap subgenre of hip-hop. This form was a reflection of "the power of negativity to keep on living in the awareness of ghetto conditions that are unlikely to be improved by government, business, or liberal whites."[22] Gangsta rap could be seen as the final "fuck you" to the white 1960s idealism, and the form "lays bare the truth that no social contract has ever existed between blacks and the United States."[23]

The lack of social contract is evident in *Colors*. The gang members have slipped to the bottom rung of the social ladder. Their only sense of belonging and status can be found within the gang context.

Two months after its release, the *Colors* soundtrack was certified gold in the United States. It was one of the first records to bring rap and hip-hop to a wider audience and to exhibit that the music had evolved to take the cultural cues, the urgency, and the DIY esthetics of punk rock and have it reflect the Black-American experience.

What became apparent after *Colors* was released was how popular hip-hop and rap music was among American audiences, particularly white suburbanites. We can use Hopper himself to demonstrate the popularity that hip-hop and rap faced in the late 1980s and 1990s. Almost exactly ten years after the release of *Colors*, Hopper appeared in a cameo role in the promotional video for rap megastar Puff Daddy's single "Victory." The single was drawn from Puff Daddy's debut album *No Way Out*, a record that has since sold over seven million copies in the United States alone. The music video was a retelling of the story of Paul Michael Glaser's 1987 film *The Running Man*, which is set within a dystopian society that is controlled by tyrannical game show hosts that keep the population distracted with images of violence, gore, and death. The original film (based on Stephen King's 1982 novel) saw Arnold Schwarzenegger playing a wrongly convicted military pilot who is forced to enter into a gruesome game show in which he must battle against a series of foes. Puff Daddy takes on the Schwarzenegger role in the video for "Victory," while Hopper plays Victor Castiglione, President of the New World Order, and orchestrator of "the game" and a heavy presence within the criminal underworld. As of this writing, the music video for "Victory" holds the title of being the tenth most expensive music promo video, with a production budget close to three million dollars.[24]

In a short expanse of time, hip-hop and rap became arguably the most dominant genre of music in the United States and beyond, influencing everything from fashion to advertisements, and a genre that major record company conglomerates would spend enormous amounts of money promoting.

Alongside the marketing of hip-hop music came the promotion of a hip-hop lifestyle, or a mutated version of gangsta style to predominantly suburban middle-class white kids. This proposed lifestyle of money, drugs, guns, flashy cars, expensive designer apparel, and promiscuous women was sold in the rhymes of rappers, in photoshoots in glossy magazines, record covers, and in X-rated music videos. The corporatization of hip-hop by record labels marketing departments thrusted an "unholy blend of ghetto fantasyland and suburban stereotype" that "reinforces the worst caricatures of gang members . . . then glamorizes them to the ghettos and barrios."[25]

Corporatized hip-hop allowed the white and wealthy suburbanites crime and poverty tourism without participation in either. They could listen, indulge in the danger, flirt with poverty, and then walk away relatively safe. It reinforced the clichés about Black, impoverished, and gang communities as violent, uneducated, and criminal. But it sent a message back to the streets that a certain lifestyle is attainable, or that it can be replicated in some way. The issue is that there is very little opportunity in simply walking away. The experience is a lived one.

The only exception to the male-dominated perspective in *Colors* is María Conchita Alonso as Louisa, but her role is reduced to a cliché sultry love interest to McGavin. Neither the script nor the direction gives her much to do with her interesting perspective as a "homegirl" looking beyond her neighborhood for a better existence. The soundtrack, however, does offer some female representation with the inclusion of all-female rap trio Salt-N-Pepa and female rapper MC Roxanne Shanté. This is notable, as Hopper's soundtracks rarely feature female artists despite the prominence of female performers in the folk and rock movement represented by *Easy Rider* and *The Last Movie* and the punk rock scene represented by *Out of the Blue*.

Colors is a male-dominated film. The two leads and the most prominent gang members are all male. Apart from Salt-N-Pepa and Roxanne Shanté, the soundtrack is male-dominated. It is worth noting that gang affiliation and the selling of the gangster lifestyle is predominantly aimed at young males who have been disadvantaged by the "deindustrialization that has devastated poor minority communities" and incapacitated young males to make them feel powerlessness, and, in turn "has led to exaggerated, defensive notions of masculinity."[26] This "exaggerated" posture is most evident in the often violent and misogynistic lyrics contained in rap music and the gratuitous nudity in music videos and on record sleeves that depict violence and sexual oppression of women. But it is important to understand that hip-hop and rap music do not breed this; the "exaggerated" posture stems, as previously discussed, from the systematic and institutional oppression of the poor and minority communities in the neoliberal hellscape. Rap artist Jay-Z notes in his introduction to Michael Eric Dyson's book *Know What I Mean?: Reflections on Hip-Hop* that

> our rhymes can contain violence and hatred. Yes, our songs can detail the drug business and our choruses can bounce with lustful intent. However, those things did not spring from inferior imaginations or deficient morals; these things came from our lives. They came from America."[27]

Hip-hop and rap music are an expression and reflection of the streets and the society one is raised in. Dyson complements Jay-Z's opening statements by exploring the lyrical tone that rap and hip-hop compositions evoke, adding that

> words are important, as a means of upward mobility, or as a means to escape suffering, especially by exposing its horrible intrusion into one's group or neighborhood, or to grapple with a white supremacist society that refuses to acknowledge our fundamental humanity.[28]

The lyrical content of rap and hip-hop music is an expression of street poetry, a method of documenting lives of people that mainstream culture ignores. As discussed, it is the television of Black America and the journalism of Black experience where none had previously existed. Dyson continues: "At its best, hip-hop grapples with politics, which is the art of making arguments over how social resources are distributed, cultural capital is accumulated, and ideological legitimacy is secured."[29] Although not explicit in the narrative of *Colors*, the use of hip-hop in the soundtrack gives the gang characters a voice with which to summarize their experiences. As Hagedorn notes, "what in fact has been going on in hip-hop culture since its creation is a vivid, no-holds-barred struggle between a host of different identities, some destructive, some liberatory, some playful, but nearly all defiant."[30]

If we did not know we were discussing hip-hop music, we could attribute the above musical descriptor to Dennis Hopper himself and all the work he has created as a film director and actor. The struggle between "different identities" has been a constant within his work, and the music selections that inhabit his films offer insight into this struggle.

With *Colors*, as with *Easy Rider*, Hopper offers a snapshot of an era through the lens of music and the connections to what might be considered a contemporary interpretation of the counterculture. Rap and hip-hop music were counter to the mainstream at this juncture. However, much like the counterculture of Hopper's iconoclast days of the late 1960s and early 1970s, rap and hip-hop would be engulfed and regurgitated by the mainstream in short order. Taken from the street corners of troubled neighborhoods and sent to the gleaming towers of New York City and Los Angeles, hip-hop and rap music would become corporatized and repackaged for the white masses. The very real disagreements and vendettas that arose between the west coast rap artists and the emerging east coast rappers became not a social issue to mediate, contain, and resolve but a marketing strategy for conglomerates to exploit. Real blood was spilled in the murders of hip-hop superstars Tupac Shakur and Notorious B.I.G., and millions of dollars were made in the process.

Notes

1 Anthony Neild, "Films for Music: Neil Young's Human Highway Reappraised," *The Quietus*, 26 April 2013 (available at https://thequietus.com/articles/11882-neil-young-human-highway-the-quietus-anthony-nield).
2 Swapnil Dhruv Bose, "The 10 Craziest Dennis Hopper Stories," *Far Out Magazine*, 17 May 2021 (available at https://faroutmagazine.co.uk/dennis-hopper-10-craziest-stories/).
3 Bill Kelly, "'Colors,' Controversy & Hopper in an Exclusive Interview – Dennis Hopper Discusses *Colors*, His Most Ambitious Filmmaking Venture since *Easy Rider*, and Reflects on Three Decades of Acting," *South Florida Sun Sentinel*, 17 April 1988 (available at www.sun-sentinel.com/news/fl-xpm-1988-04-17-8801240357-story.html).
4 Hal Hinson, "Colors," *Washington Post*, 15 April 1988 (available at www.washingtonpost.com/wp-srv/style/longterm/movies/videos/colorsrhinson_a0c902.htm).
5 Matthieu Orléan, "Photography, Writing, Acting . . . Movie-Making had Everything in One Package: Interview with Dennis Hopper," in *Dennis Hopper and the New Hollywood* (Paris: Flammarion, 2008), 139.
6 Kelly, "'Colors,' Controversy & Hopper."
7 Ibid.
8 Hinson, "Colors."
9 Aaron Rose, "The Unvisual City," in *Dennis Hopper: Colors. The Polaroids* (Bologna: Damiani, 2016), page numbers unspecified.
10 Andrew Goodwin, *Dancing in the Distraction Factory: Music Television and Popular Culture* (Minneapolis: University of Minnesota Press, 1993), 59.

11 Mike Davis, *Foreword to A World of Gangs: Armed Young Men and Gangsta Culture* (Minneapolis: University of Minnesota Press, 2009), xi.
12 Rosa Sanchez, "Police, Residents Plead for Ceasefire after South LA Sees 59 Shooting Victims in 1st 2 Weeks of 2021," *ABC News*, 23 January 2021 (available at https://abcnews.go.com/US/police-ceasefire-south-la-sees-59-shooting-victims/story?id=75441899).
13 Kelly, "'Colors,' Controversy & Hopper."
14 Albert Auster and Leonard Quart, *American Film and Society Since 1945* (Santa Barbara: Praeger, 2011), 159.
15 Sheila Benson, "Complexity and Context Washed Out of 'Colors'," *Los Angeles Times*, 15 April 1988 (available at www.latimes.com/archives/la-xpm-1988-04-15-ca-1305-story.html).
16 Kelly, "'Colors,' Controversy & Hopper."
17 Ibid.
18 John Hagedorn, *A World of Gangs: Armed Young Men and Gangsta Culture* (Minneapolis: University of Minnesota Press, 2008), 57.
19 Ibid.
20 Ibid.
21 Ibid., 96.
22 Ibid., 98.
23 Derrick Darby and Tommie Shelby, *Hip Hop and Philosophy: Rhyme 2 Reason* (Chicago: Open Court, 2005), 175.
24 The "Victory" promotional video was directed by Marcus Nispel and featured a cameo from Danny DeVito. The song also features Busta Rhymes and the late The Notorious B.I.G. The video can be viewed at www.youtube.com/watch?v=LsjWko_fqus.
25 Hagedorn, *A World of Gangs*, 105.
26 Ibid., 103.
27 Jay-Z, *Introduction to Know What I Mean?: Reflections on Hip-Hop* (New York: Civitas Books, 2007), x.
28 Michael Eric Dyson, *Know What I Mean?: Reflections on Hip-Hop* (New York: Civitas Books, 2007), 76.
29 Dyson, *Know What I Mean?*, 82.
30 Hagedorn, *A World of Gangs*, 102.

5 Blue Notes

Jazz and Blues Music Hybridity, and (Mis)Representation of Black Voices in *The Hot Spot*

It would appear Dennis Hopper's preference for soundtracking his films is to create a compilation of preexisting music and popular songs and incorporate them (with some exception) into the narrative as non-diegetic music. He contradicts this with his sixth film, *The Hot Spot* (1990). Hopper assigned a composer and a group of musicians to produce a full and original score for the film. No popular works were used; there was no lyrical emphasis to give voice to the characters' interior motives. If there is one thing this book has raised, it is that Hopper's lack of consistency, self-contradiction, and desire to attempt something innovative and exciting are his most interesting attributes.

The Hot Spot is remembered (if it even is at all) as a raunchy potboiler neo-noir film. It is certainly Hopper's most extravagant film in terms of its cast, which includes Don Johnson, Jennifer Connelly, and Virginia Madsen, and character actors Jack Nance and William Sadler in supporting roles. As with *Colors*, Hopper remains behind the camera to focus on the direction alone.

Hopper, with the assistance of American composer Jack Nitzsche, commissioned an original soundtrack that features a collaboration between jazz musician Miles Davis and blues guitarist and vocalist John Lee Hooker. Playing within the session is multi-instrumentalist Taj Mahal, bassist Tim Drummond, and drummer Earl Palmer. The ensemble creates an original score of free-flowing, steamy jazz, and blues hybrid compositions.

The Hot Spot is an adaptation of author Charles Williams's 1952 pulp fiction novel, *Hell Hath No Fury*. Williams had adapted the book decades earlier as a vehicle for Robert Mitchum, but the script had been shelved and forgotten until Hopper and his production partner Paul Lewis rediscovered it. As usual, the drama common to a Hopper production persisted. A screenplay titled *The Hot Spot*, written by screenwriter and filmmaker Mike Figgis, was originally intended as a high-octane heist movie, but as Don Johnson noted this script was abandoned "three days before we started shooting," with Hopper calling a meeting of the cast and passing around the Charles Williams screenplay stating: "We're not making that script. We're making this one."[1] The uneasiness between director and cast continued even after the film had wrapped, with Johnson and Madsen not participating in the promotional rounds.

DOI: 10.4324/9781003465843-6

The Hot Spot comes directly from the era in which the source material was written. Hopper himself dubbed the film a "Last Tango in Texas . . . a very seedy, sultry, hot piece,"[2] and that seems a valid assessment. Hopper creates an enjoyable, if slightly long-winded film (at 130 minutes, it is Hopper's longest) that has an atmosphere of sassy intrigue, artistic pretensions, and adequate performances in line with the material.

The narrative centers on drifter Harry Madox (Johnson), who stumbles into a small Texan town and takes a job as a car salesman. He becomes involved with two women, the sweet and innocent Gloria Harper (Connelly), a secretary at the car dealership, and Dolly Harshaw (Madsen), a femme fatale who is married to the dealership's owner. Harry's past is not alluded to, though we are made aware that he is an out of luck con man of sorts. He devises a plan to rob the local bank, which is staffed by workers who also happen to be volunteer firefighters. He ignites a fire in a disused building across the street from the bank; this clears the bank tellers and allows Harry the time to then stroll in, casually empty the cash drawers, and leave town to start a new life for himself and Gloria. Things do not go to plan and Dolly, knowing of his crimes, bribes Harry into an unhappy life with her.

Unlike films that fall into the genre of noir, in which the action plays out in shadows and darkness, *The Hot Spot* is full of bright light and vivid color. Hopper leads the direction in a "tough and stylish" manner but is countered by the "sunny look of Ueli Steiger's cinematography."[3] A sense of oppressive Texan heat hangs over the film as characters sweat through their suits and dresses and fans continuously whirl in order to cool down the boiling hot rooms. The heat never seems to dissipate even when it rains. The film shares more with the popular neo-noir of the era such as David Lynch's *Wild at Heart* (1990), John Dahl's *Red Rock West* (1993), and Oliver Stone's *Natural Born Killers* (1994). In these films, the protagonists blur the line, and in some cases cross it fully into antagonist territory.

The Hot Spot is a contemporary-set film, yet the town has regressed to the 1950s or the place simply never moved on from that decade. The clothes, the cars, the houses, and the mannerisms all recall that period in this pocket of the Southern States. Hopper has situated his film within the same small American town that *Easy Rider*'s Billy and Wyatt roll through when they join the parade and get locked up in the local jail for being "longhairs." Their cellmate George Hanson explains that the town folks have a "scissor-happy, beautify America thing" going on, in which "they're tryin' to make everybody look like Yul Brynner." Hopper uses Hanson's description of small-town America as his base location. No long hair, no hippies, no prominent Black folk. No children are seen or alluded to. Sometimes the town even looks deserted of people altogether.

Hopper lets us know that we are in a contemporary setting through the soundtrack alone. When Madox first arrives in town, he enters a strip bar that is playing Billy Squier's thumping 1981 rock anthem "The Stroke," while dancers perform for the male patrons. In a later scene in the same club, we hear

Figure 5.1 The rock music that plays in the seedy strip bar on the rundown side of town is the only indication that *The Hot Spot* is a contemporary story.

Source: *The Hot Spot*

Hank Williams, Jr.'s, 1988 hit "Love M.D." When Harry exits the bar and steps across the street toward the car dealership, we are transported back in time. The owner George Harshaw (Jerry Hardin) and his associate Lon (Charles Martin Smith) are both dressed in 1950s garb: high-waist suit pants, skinny neckties, cowboy boots, and hats. The music also shifts to the laid-back groove of John Lee Hooker's crooning voice and Miles Davis' lazy and wandering trumpet. Madox returns to the club on several occasions, with always the same kind of 1980s hard rock music blaring. It is an odd and destabilizing use of music styles and the only way that Hopper informs the audience of *The Hot Spot*'s actual time frame.

The film has two minor Black characters. One of these is American bluesman Roosevelt "Grey Ghost" Williams, who jams out live renditions of his songs "Lonesome Traveller" and "You're Nobody till Somebody Loves You" on a piano in the film's background. Both these songs relate to Harry's predicament; *he* is a "lonesome traveler" and a "nobody" until Gloria and Dolly take an interest in him. Oddly, Williams does not appear on the main soundtrack, as his piano-led blues would have been perfectly suitable and would have offered some variation alongside Davis' horn and Hooker's guitar. The other Black character is Uncle Mort (John Hawker), an elderly blind man who will be discussed shortly as his role relates to an interesting moment within the film and soundtrack.

Despite the visual lack of representation, the music of the soundtrack is unequivocally Black in origin and performance. Davis's horn and Hooker's guitar and vocals encircle each other like roaming buffalo readying to tackle each other on the hot plains – neither attacks. The compositions do not take off in a musical sense. They instead hover in a liminal space, never leaving their destination and never arriving; they are, as Ben Watson notes, like "sex that never comes."[4] The compositions seem like well-produced mood pieces, or sketches of something that never quite emerges. This is not to suggest that the music does not live up to the legends performing it. Each composition has, as Steve Day notes in his critique, a "simplicity" that "hurts long after you have finished hearing it."[5] Indeed, the music leaves the listener on the yearning precipice of wanting to hear more.

    Hopper had the idea to merge jazz and blues, and he placed the project in the hands of composer and record producer Jack Nitzsche. Nitzsche and Hopper had known each other for decades after meeting on the set of *Easy Rider* when Nitzsche's friend and record-producing partner Phil Spector made a brief cameo as the drug buyer who puts Billy and Wyatt on the road to financial independence. Nitzsche had produced records for The Rolling Stones and Neil Young, and he had composed award-nominated scores for films such as Miloš Forman's *One Flew Over the Cuckoo's Nest* (1975), Paul Schrader's *Blue Collar* (1978), Taylor Hackford's *An Officer and a Gentleman* (1982), and John Carpenter's *Starman* (1984). According to the liner notes for *The Hot Spot*'s soundtrack, Hopper had met Miles Davis when he was just 17 years old when Davis had "punched out" Hopper's heroin dealer and threatened Hopper if he ever touched the stuff again. Hopper's liner notes also suggest that he had wanted Davis to score all of his past directorial films. Thinking over this prospect leaves one to wonder how *Easy Rider* or *Out of the Blue* would have been received with a jazz score underpinning Billy and Wyatt's cross-country journey, or Cebe's excursion to the big city.

    Continuing his analysis of *The Hot Spot*'s soundtrack, Steve Day notes that "these are not so much songs {as] they are vocal riffs rubbed along the surface of music"; he states, too, that the session that produced these notes feels "moody, bleak rough-reel,"[6] and that Hooker's yearning, soulful, moanin' and groanin' voice gives the music a beautiful yet terrible depth, the sound of a man in the throes of undeniable (and unbearable) passion. Day remarks that Davis' horn "slithers forth across the oh-so-basic tin bath, twelve-bar blues structures, somehow making each [note] an invitation to the very heart of his genius."[7] Day's critique points toward an obvious truth. Hooker's compositions are dark, quiet, and incredibly simplistic; Davis offers the flickers of light and a way in for the listener to connect. It is, as Day comments, "the personification of the blues struck through by a jazz master beating the air with the deliberate act of acid in your heart."[8]

    Listening to the soundtrack isolated from the film's visuals, one can picture and sense that the session that produced it must have been loose, fun, relaxed, and hazy with smoke. Unlike previous Hopper soundtracks that have relied on the differing genres of the compilation format, *The Hot Spot* soundtrack has a unified feel, a single movement that glides gently along the narrative lines of the film where "the unhurried vamps drift along, luring the musicians into wonderfully open, exploratory tangents that sometimes go nowhere and sometimes wind up in unexpectedly poignant places."⁹

There is a sense that Hopper wanted the soundtrack of *The Hot Spot* to linger in the background. His films before this had ensured that the soundtrack held relevance, distinction, and noticeability. Here, the score drifts in and out, remaining but not intruding upon the scenes. The music does not speak for or reflect any character emotion. Its purpose is to just sit and simmer in the background. As a movement of music, it is an interesting and alluring concoction; as a soundtrack to a Dennis Hopper movie, it fails to make the all-important cultural connections and insinuations standard to a Hopper-directed film.

The only time the music seems to react is when Harry is orchestrating the bank robbery and emptying the cash drawers. A lone Black and visually impaired gentleman, referred to as Uncle Mort, enters in search of the bank's manager (Jack Nance), who is tied up and gagged in the washroom. The musical score has a "pounding train time blues" feel that sees bass player Tim Drummond "hitting a tremulous three-note riff, the notes flexing like muscles" while Hooker's guitar spits with "splintered anger."¹⁰ As Harry and Mort face each other the music abruptly pauses, with only Hooker's vocal hum continuing under the tense moment. When Harry slips by the man unnoticed, the band kicks in again as Harry flees the scene.

Krin Gabbard commented on this scene in his essay "White Face, Black Noise: Miles Davis and the Soundtrack," noting that it "is especially intriguing that the blind man is black," and he suggests that "the blindness of the audience toward blacks on the soundtrack is displaced onto the black man."¹¹ This

Figure 5.2 Despite the prominent use of jazz and blues music from two leading Black musicians, the only Black character within the entire film is a blind man.

Source: *The Hot Spot*

is an interesting assessment of not just this scene but the *entire* soundtrack, and a majority of Hollywood films that flesh out the white perspectives of the narratives with compositions written and performed by Black musicians. A clear example is John Landis's film *The Blues Brothers* (1980), which featured two white protagonists performing music originally composed by Black blues musicians.

There is also an example from Hopper's 1988 film *Colors*. Hopper's embrace of a predominantly Black form of musical style, this being hip-hop and rap music, does not necessarily reflect the perspective of the film's protagonists, nor the film's outlook. He makes a similar decision with *The Hot Spot* soundtrack by using a predominantly Black musical ensemble to help illustrate a story of all-white sexual politics and lustful betrayal.

As discussed, Hopper's soundtracks are male-centric in the artists featured and the viewpoint the compositions take. In this respect, *The Hot Spot* soundtrack is the guiltiest in Hopper's filmography. The film takes the vantage point of "a roadhouse-mentality depiction of women,"[12] yet the soundtrack is devoid of female representation. In the same fashion that *Out of the Blue*'s Cebe is soundtracked by male artists, Dolly and Gloria are attributed musical notes directly from the instruments of Black male musicians.

It has been noted that Dennis Hopper's directorial films contain a central ideological struggle, a "clash between irreconcilable viewpoints and lifestyles," the hippies vs. the squares, the punks vs. the boomers, the gangs vs. the cops, "and, increasingly in the later work, females [vs.] males."[13] *The Hot Spot*, and Hopper's 1994 follow-up, *Chasers*, certainly support this later notion. Both films pit male and female protagonists against each other in a battle of the sexes. The cultural battles that outlined Hopper's earlier work are mostly absent from these later films. Without that cultural tension at play, Hopper's work becomes muted. The soundtracks might have stepped in to negotiate this if the narrative was not outwardly commenting on events (as it did with *Easy Rider*), but with *The Hot Spot* we are left with an awkward admission that the soundtrack is the most exceptional aspect of the film. And though the music simmers and sizzles it is far from the best work that any of those involved committed to record. In regard to action on screen, *The Hot Spot* is Hopper's quietest and most subtle film.

Notes

1 Will Harris, "Don Johnson on Cold in July, Dennis Hopper, and auditioning for Miami Vice," *AV Club*, 30 May 2014 (available at www.avclub.com/don-johnson-on-cold-in-july-dennis-hopper-and-auditio-1798269633).
2 Donna Rosenthal, "Hopper's Odyssey – From Hell to Texas: Dennis Hopper has Experienced Acting Success, Druggy Exile, Psychiatric Wards and Now He's Directing 'Hot Spot'," *Los Angeles Times*, 5 November 1989 (available at www.latimes.com/archives/la-xpm-1989-11-05-ca-1727-story.html).

3 Janet Maslin, "Taxidermy and Temptations: Dennis Hopper's Dark World," *New York Times*, 12 October 1990 (available at www.nytimes.com/1990/10/12/movies/reviews-film-taxidermy-and-temptations-dennis-hopper-s-dark-world.html).
4 Ben Watson, *Honesty is Explosive!: Selected Music Journalism* (San Bernardino: Bongo Press, 2010), 15.
5 Steve Day, "Miles Davis & John Lee Hooker: *The Hot Spot*," *Sandy Brown Jazz*, 2016–2017 (available at www.sandybrownjazz.co.uk/FullFocus/TheHotSpot.html).
6 Ibid.
7 Ibid.
8 Ibid.
9 Ibid.
10 Watson, *Honesty is Explosive!* 14.
11 Krin Gabbard, "White Face, Black Noise: Miles Davis and the Soundtrack," in *Beyond the Soundtrack: Representing Music in Cinema*, ed. Daniel Goldmark, Lawrence Kramer, and Richard Leppert (Los Angeles: University of California Press, 2007), 266–67.
12 Desson Howe, "Hopper Marks 'The Hot Spot'," *Washington Post*, 26 October 1990 (available at www.washingtonpost.com/archive/lifestyle/1990/10/26/hopper-marks-the-hot-spot/267b629a-78af-410a-9303-3b76813ac0a0/).
13 Brad Stevens, "Dennis Hopper: The Last Director," *British Film Institute: Sight and Sound*, 22 September 2015 (available at https://www2.bfi.org.uk/news-opinion/sight-sound-magazine/comment/obituaries/dennis-hopper-last-director).

Conclusion

In a 2008 advertisement campaign for Orange cell phones, Dennis Hopper, in a comedic take on his bomb terrorist character from *Speed* (1994), apprehends two movie executives on a city bus and spins them a pitch for a movie he wishes to direct. The synopsis concerns a city stockbroker who loses everything in a market crash and must take a city bus every morning to his new menial job. Forced to confront diverse cultures and socioeconomic perspectives, the broker's life is turned around. Of course, as was the norm with this series of advertisements, the movie executives try to place the Orange cell phone as a key narrative tool, much to Hopper's clear annoyance. An aspect of the advert that strikes me is why Hopper did not ever make the film he proposed. Why did he not create smaller films that were snippets of American life?

Dennis Hopper should have directed more than just seven feature films. When asked about upcoming film projects in interviews post-1986, there always seemed to be some directorial possibility on the horizon and always some project that had been abandoned. For example, Hopper had an opportunity to direct Sean Penn in the Charles Bukowski-penned screenplay for *Barfly* (1987). The deal fell through, and the film would eventually surface with director Barbet Schroeder with Mickey Rourke as the lead actor. There was even talk, sometime in the early 1980s, of a sequel to *Easy Rider*, titled *Bikers Heaven*, that would have resurrected Billy and Wyatt in Reagan's America. A sequel became a reality in 2012 with Dustin Rikert's *Easy Rider 2: The Ride Home*; this film, a strange revisionist, conservative, and oddly pro-war take on the original film, generated little fanfare, and none of the original cast or crew were involved. Hopper's reliance on Hollywood to finance and release his films was maybe the obstacle he placed in front of himself. He could have found financing from the independent film sector and opted for a more low-budget method of film production. If he had done this, we would certainly have more work to ponder. His most expensive movie was *Chasers*, with a fifteen million budget. After it bombed both critically and commercially, it was also his last feature-length film.

DOI: 10.4324/9781003465843-7

Conclusion 65

After the success of *Easy Rider*, Hopper broke ranks with his fellow New Hollywood directors and went with a major studio for his next film. His cohort – including Bob Rafelson, Peter Bogdanovich, Henry Jaglom, and Jack Nicholson – went on to direct films with the independent BBS Productions, a company that evolved from the Raybert Productions that had produced *Easy Rider*.

While Hopper's own directorial career fell by the wayside in the post-New Hollywood era and later in the mid-1990s, other filmmakers of the time took the cues from *Easy Rider* and *Colors* in soundtracking their films the way Hopper had and used compilation-style soundtracks of already recorded and popular songs.

There is a distinct division in Hopper's directorial work. His first four films offer a dark interpretation of American life, his last three films less so. This is apparent in the stories he chose to tell in those last three films *Catchfire*, *The Hot Spot*, and *Chasers*. Societal and political critique in these films is all but abandoned. Although *Catchfire* contains meditations on art and commerce, the focus is on human relationships, predominantly between male and female. The music and soundtracks in these last three films, while certainly adequate and complementary to the story, say very little.

Hopper's directorial career and his soundtracking techniques have been applied by subsequent filmmakers to create their own glimpses of American culture in independent cinema. We can see this in the work of auteur filmmakers such as Jim Jarmusch, Sean Penn, Cameron Crowe, Gus Van Sant, Jason Reitman, Richard Linklater, Vincent Gallo, Andrew Bujalski, Sofia Coppola, Quintin Tarantino, Lynn Shelton, Kelly Reichardt, and Alex Ross Perry, among many others. These filmmakers make small, independently produced, and released films that include popular music or musical performances. Through lyrics and familiarity, the compilation soundtrack has become a signature for filmmakers to make instantaneous emotional connections with the audience. And the impact is not just felt within independent cinema. One need only look to the big-budget *Guardians of the Galaxy* films, directed by James Gunn, within the Marvel Cinematic Universe, to find an example of the compilation soundtrack.

Upon investigating Hopper's directorial films through the lens of their soundtracks, something becomes clear. His work, while interesting and engaging, and certainly adequate in terms of film language, and able to garner a cult following, does not quite reach the giddy emotional heights of Stanley Kubrick, Martin Scorsese, Terrence Malick, Jean-Luc Godard, François Truffaut, Orson Welles, or Elia Kazan. Hopper may have adored the work of the auteurs of the French New Wave and the experimental films of Bruce Conner and Andy Warhol, and would use their methods in his own films, but he shared more with the straightforward and simplistic narrative style of Hollywood pros like John Ford,

George Stevens, or Henry Hathaway. For Hopper, a "child of the studio system," after all, may "have been both that system's greatest enemy and its most passionate champion."[1] The straightforward directing style can be found in the fixed camera positions in *Out of the Blue*, and one could argue that *Easy Rider* is for all intents and purposes a western with motorcycles in place of steeds.

Hopper's directorial films concisely critique the social, political, and cultural climates of the late twentieth century. Through his narratives, Hopper weaves threads of what was laying waste to the fabric of the so-called American Dream, and after *Easy Rider* he used his films to further document the death knell of American life. As Hopper once commented: "All my films end in fire."[2] Hopper saw that the future of American exceptionalism was in decline and that societal and cultural degradation was inevitable. The youth was in revolt. Burn it all down – why not?

His critique was not always explicit, and oftentimes was of only small concern. *Easy Rider*'s commentary that America was going to hell came from the perspective of two hippie outcasts unwilling to engage with society. *The Last Movie* made insinuations that the gratuitous sex and violence present in Hollywood movies and the glorification of death were having an adverse, desensitizing effect on the minds of its audiences. *Out of the Blue* explored the disintegration of the nuclear family unit and the nihilism of youth culture in the late 1970s and early 1980s as punk and disco music swept the nation. The same could be said of *Colors*, where the family unit has been obliterated and replaced with gang affiliation, urban decay, warfare, and survival on the streets. Perhaps these threads only apply to the first four of Hopper's seven films, and as he attempted to "simplify and romanticize" his work, as he had commented his intentions on *The Merv Griffin Show* in 1971, he diluted his stance to create entertainment. The soundtrack deficiency in his last three films supports this idea. Music supplied the critique in the first four films; in the last three films, it does not. The marriage of images and music in those first four films offers a more radical reading than would have been the case without the soundtracks or associations with certain music cultures. This can be witnessed in *Easy Rider* as a most obvious example. Without its soundtrack pulling from contemporary songs of the era and being joined with the exquisite cinematography of Lázló Kovács, a less powerful, and certainly less culturally significant film would exist. Without its soundtrack, audiences would probably recall *Easy Rider* simply as a more meditative and more expertly photographed exploitation biker film.

Out of the Blue benefits from its association with punk rock even though it only includes a handful of actual punk music within its soundtrack from the diegetic live performances of The Pointed Sticks. *Colors* uses an association with hip-hop, rap, and gang culture to reposition a standard police procedural drama as a study of life for Black people. In each instance we see the soundtrack come out on top and become essential element to the overall experience.

This is not to suggest that without a song-based soundtrack Dennis Hopper's directional work lacks excitement. Yet we see that music and sound improved

Hopper's images greatly. One example of a "musicless" film in Hopper's directorial arsenal is the nine-minute digital film *Homeless* (2000). This was Hopper's final directorial work, and certainly his least remarkable. Conceived as part of an abandoned online film festival that Hopper and Quentin Tarantino were set to judge, the film has instead been integrated into his artistic works, usually being shown on a loop during gallery exhibitions.

The film follows a day in the life of a young homeless woman as she pushes her grocery cart of belongings around a nameless town. Flashbacks show us her days as an exotic dancer. The film is mostly a montage of images, with no dialogue and, as noted, no examples of popular music. The only sound is the rumble of cars and buses and indistinct conversations from people as they pass the woman in the street. It becomes noticeably clear that while Hopper was excited by the accessibility, ease of movement, quick results, and fast editing turnaround of digital film, the results speak differently. The color, vibrancy, and overall excitement of a Hopper film are absent here, replaced by the dull, flat murkiness of digital film. What is even more apparent is that with no music to accompany the images, or to give voice to the homeless woman, there is no sympathetic development made with the audience. The character is given no inner life; where music and sound may have filled that void, we are given nothing to ponder.

This can also be witnessed in Hopper's fifth film *Catchfire* (1990), which features a rudimentary and unmemorable score by composers Curt Sobel and Michel Colombier that plays on the noir elements of the narrative. *Catchfire* is a well-crafted crime thriller with a comedic edge that shows some eccentricity and artistic flair with the inclusion of works by neo-conceptual artist Jenny Holzer as a plot device, and some stunning location work on Hopper's Taos compound. A soundtrack that expressed aplomb might have given the film a more exciting flow and may have been more favorably received by critics and audiences. The film is one that Hopper openly rejected. It is obvious that its weakness is a lack of a vibrant soundtrack to complement its imagery and off-kilter performances.

An aspect of Dennis Hopper's persona that has intrigued me is the level of discovery that awaits anyone who engages with his work and the way his art echoes throughout the eras and reflects, and therefore affects, different generations. My journey began with *Easy Rider* and the surrounding counterculture the film represented. I continued to be thrilled (and unnerved) by Hopper's performances in *Blue Velvet*, and *River's Edge*. This led to discovering more mainstream films that he had appeared in such as *Speed* and *Waterworld* (1995), moving onto the more low-profile films such as the Australian bizarro bushranger adventure *Mad Dog Morgan* (1976), the Patricia Highsmith adaptation *The American Friend* (1977) set in West Germany and directed by Wim Wenders, and Roland Klick's *White Star* (1983). The oddest of these foreign films is *Bloodbath* (also known as *The Sky is Falling*, and as *Las Flores Del Vicio*), a strange surrealist film set in Spain and made by Canadian director Silvio Narizzano. Unable to secure decent roles in American films, Hopper found opportunities everywhere, creating an extremely interesting "lost" period of films from 1972 to 1984 that are worthy of investigation. Hopper's film work led me to discover his art and photography, which led me deeper into the cultural impact of his life and times as a whole. With thanks to the emergence of online streaming platforms, a never-ending rabbit-hole of interviews, film scenes, and performances, moments from Hopper's artistic existence opened up.

The discovery is far from over. Photographs from Hopper's archives are being uncovered and released in monographs, most recently *Dennis Hopper: Colors, The Polaroids*, and *Dennis Hopper: In Dreams: Scenes from the Archive*. Art and photographic exhibitions continue to be displayed worldwide. *The Last Movie* and *Out of the Blue* have been given extensive restorations and re-released to cinemas, screened at film festivals, and released on DVD/Blu-Ray. Recently discovered footage of an extensive conversation between Hopper and director Orson Welles has been issued as a two-hour feature-length documentary, titled *Hopper/Welles* (2022), that uncovers the nature of film and life from both directors' perspectives. *Hopper/Welles* also ties in with Hopper's appearance in Welles's long-lost film *The Other Side of the Wind* (2018), which started production in the early 1970s and became mythic in its absence. The film finally saw the light of day after a successful campaign to raise funds to complete the production.

In the last few years, associates of Dennis Hopper have made in-depth and intriguing documentaries on his legacy. The first of these was German film director Hermann Vaske's documentary film *Uneasy Rider* (2016); Hopper's personal assistant Satya De La Manitou teamed with director Nick Ebeling for *Along for the Ride* (2016), perhaps the most in-depth exploration of Hopper's life, times and impact, with an explicit focus on *The Last Movie*. An extensive companion book has also been issued.

There is now Hopper-branded apparel and Hopper-branded cannabis that taps into the spirit of independence, rebelliousness, and artistic freedom bestowed on the culture in 1969 when he, Fonda, and Nicholson lit up a joint around the campfire in *Easy Rider* and committed to screen one of the funniest and most naturalistic scenes in cinema.

Then there are his film soundtracks, the research of which opens further avenues of intrigue. I have maintained focus on Dennis Hopper's work by looking at him and observing his performances in films. Not an actor known for nuances (though they exist, and they are admirable), in all his roles he exhibits exuberant mannerisms and often loud, operatic, and precise ways of speaking lines. Delving into the songs and music that populate Hopper's directorial films reveals a director in constant conversation with the culture surrounding him. The nuance is to be found in the soundtracks. It is not accidental. It is carefully considered.

A Dennis Hopper soundtrack is a crucial element of the experience. Hopper recognized that incorporating a soundtrack bursting with iconic songs into *Easy Rider* would add cultural weight to the film. Hopper never shied away from experimentation, and his musical soundtrack choices reflect this. Even *Easy Rider*'s more mainstream musical selections of Bob Dylan, The Byrds, and Steppenwolf are contrasted with experimental folk from The Holy Modal Rounders and psychedelic rock band The Electric Prunes. In *Out of the Blue*, Hopper's use of insinuations with punk rock gives the film an urgency that makes the music a vital piece of punk filmmaking. The use of rap and hip-hop music in *Colors* was significant to the characters of the film and a cultural reflection of the time in which it was made. The upcoming wave of rap and hip-hop was to signal one of the most important and iconic shifts in American music and culture since the 1960s.

Although they were writing about musicians and bands when they proposed the idea, the late cultural theorist Mark Fisher, along with critic Simon Reynolds, talked about the notion of "portal bands" or "portal artists" that through their lyrics or esthetics led the listener toward a world of discovery. Fisher states that bands such as the Sex Pistols, The Fall, and Public Enemy did not change the world through a declaration of war or revolution but by "intervening in everyday life," and that these artists

> offered a puncturing, a rupture of the accepted structure of reality. The puncture would produce a portal – an escape route from the second-nature habits of everyday life into a new labyrinth of associations and connections, where politics would connect with art and theory in unexpected ways.[3]

I would apply Fisher's observation to the entire work of Dennis Hopper. His existence bridged art and film through his activity as a photographer, artist, and art collector and his work as a film director and film actor. His "associations and connections" are limitless, but the worlds were not separate. They merge into a whole and exist as one. The music he selected for his soundtracks is an important aspect of understanding this as they connect the art with the political. They lead the listener/viewer to further engage with the films and go beyond what is just presented on screen. The soundtrack of *Easy Rider* is such a staple of the 1960s sound that one cannot help but dive deeper into the decade to explore the radical and progressive movements that spawned, thrived, or disintegrated before the decade was over. My own journey from *Easy Rider* drew me toward the music and lives of Bob Dylan, the Doors, and Tim Buckley, to the writings of Hunter S. Thompson and Jack Kerouac and the Beat Generation. It also led me to exploring New Hollywood cinema, the avant-garde, and the British New Wave. This one film, a small but potent offering within New Hollywood, offered an immense opportunity for education and realization.

The soundtrack to *Colors* allows listeners a glimpse of life within the gang cultures of Los Angeles but heading further into the "portal" leads one to recognize the raw deal that Black Americans and other minority groups have been dealt by American society at large. The hip-hop genre is a symbol of this dissolution and harks back to the Black radical movements of the 1960s, Malcolm

X, and the Black Panthers, and artists such as The Last Poets and Gil Scott Heron. The soundtrack to *Colors* led me to other rap and hip-hop artists such as Public Enemy and N.W.A., and to critics such as Michael Eric Dyson and Mike Davis, who explored and deciphered the cultural importance of hip-hop and urban existence in Los Angeles and beyond. It was not just me who felt this way. Hopper's *Easy Rider* costar Peter Fonda wrote a short in-memoriam to Hopper for *Time* magazine in which he stated:

> Dennis Hopper took me on a journey. It was with him that I found myself in the studios and dining rooms of the top modern artists in the U.S. – Ed Kienholz, Ed Ruscha, Jasper Johns, Roy Lichtenstein. It was with him that I found my way to the Pasadena art museum, screening old, forgotten films from great directors. It was Dennis who put me together with Bruce Conner, a genius collage artist and filmmaker who greatly influenced the films I have directed.

Fonda signed off his piece with: "Dennis always percolates deep in my soul."[4] I perceive Hopper the same way, and it is the union of sound and images that have made this connection enduring. Hopper placed some of the most important music and music cultures within his films. If the soundtracks of *Easy Rider*, *The Last Movie*, *The American Dreamer*, *Out of the Blue*, *Colors*, and *The Hot Spot* offered such an education as to how music and sound can relate to the culture and politics of their times, then imagine what an entire life could teach. Dennis Hopper's life *is* that life.

Notes

1 Brad Stevens, "Dennis Hopper: The Last Director," *British Film Institute: Sight and Sound*, 22 September 2015 (available at https://www2.bfi.org.uk/news-opinion/sight-sound-magazine/comment/obituaries/dennis-hopper-last-director).
2 Chuck Stephens, "Death's Angel: Peter Fonda in *Easy Rider*," *Criterion*, 4 September 2019 (available at www.criterion.com/current/posts/6572-death-s-angel-peter-fonda-in-easy-rider).
3 Mark Fisher, *K-Punk: The Collected and Unpublished Writings of Mark Fisher (2004–2016)* (London: Repeater Books, 2018), 383.
4 Peter Fonda, "Person of the Year 2010," *Time Magazine*, 15 December 2010 (available at http://content.time.com/time/specials/packages/article/0,28804,2036683_2036477_2036464,00.html).

Bibliography

Almereyda, Michael, "Fade Out: Dennis Hopper," *Film Comment*. Available at www.filmcomment.com/article/fade-out-michael-almereyda-on-dennis-hopper/.
Auster, Albert and Quart, Leonard, *American Film and Society Since 1945*. Santa Barbara: Praeger, 2011.
Becker, Carol, *The Subversive Imagination: Artists, Society & Social Responsibility*. New York: Routledge, 1994.
Benson, Sheila, "Complexity and Context Washed Out of 'Colors'," *Los Angeles Times*. Available at www.latimes.com/archives/la-xpm-1988-04-15-ca-1305-story.html.
Bose, Swapnil Dhruv, "The 10 Craziest Dennis Hopper Stories," *Far Out Magazine*. Available at https://faroutmagazine.co.uk/dennis-hopper-10-craziest-stories/.
Brandum, Dean, "A Legacy Went Searching for a Film . . . Dennis Hopper and Easy Rider," *Senses of Cinema*. Available at www.sensesofcinema.com/2010/feature-articles/a-legacy-went-searching-for-a-film%E2%80%A6-dennis-hopper-and-easy-rider/.
Brant, Peter M. and Shafrazi, Tony, "Dennis Hopper Part Two," *Interview Magazine*. Available at www.interviewmagazine.com/film/dennis-hopper-part-two.
Cole, Toby and Chinoy, Helen Krich, *Actors on Acting: The Theories, Techniques, and Practises of the World's Great Actors, Told in Their Own Words*. New York: Three Rivers Press, 1995.
Colley, Iain, *Film Notes: 'Easy Rider'*. London: Longman, 2000.
Darby, Derrick and Shelby, Tommie, *Hip Hop and Philosophy: Rhyme 2 Reason*. Chicago: Open Court, 2005.
Davis, Mike, *Foreword to A World of Gangs: Armed Young Men and Gangsta Culture*. Minneapolis: University of Minnesota Press, 2009.
Day, Steve, "Miles Davis & John Lee Hooker: The Hot Spot," *Sandy Brown Jazz*. Available at www.sandybrownjazz.co.uk/FullFocus/TheHotSpot.html.
Dyson, Michael Eric, *Know What I Mean?: Reflections on Hip-Hop*. New York: Civitas Books, 2007.
Ebert, Roger, "The Last Movie / Chincero Movie Review," *Rogerebert.Com*, 1971. Available at www.rogerebert.com/reviews/the-last-movie – chinchero-1971.
Fisher, Mark, *K-Punk: The Collected and Unpublished Writings of Mark Fisher*. London: Repeater Books, 2018.

Fonda, Peter, "Person of the Year 2010," *Time Magazine*. Available at http://content.time.com/time/specials/packages/article/0,28804,2036683_2036477_2036464,00.html.

Gabbard, Krin, "White Face, Black Noise: Miles Davis and the Soundtrack," in *Beyond the Soundtrack: Representing Music in Cinema*, ed. Daniel Goldmark, Lawrence Kramer, and Richard Leppert. Los Angeles: University of California Press, 2007.

Goodwin, Andrew, *Dancing in the Distraction Factory: Music Television and Popular Culture*. Minneapolis: University of Minnesota Press, 1992.

Greiving, Tim, "Easy Rider at 50: How Groundbreaking Soundtrack Came Together," *Los Angeles Times*. Available at www.latimes.com/entertainment-arts/movies/story/2019-08-09/easy-rider-at-50-how-they-put-together-that-groundbreaking-soundtrack.

Hagedorn, John, *A World of Gangs: Armed Young Men and Gangsta Culture*. Minneapolis: University of Minnesota Press, 2008.

Harris, Will, "Don Johnson on Cold in July, Dennis Hopper, and Auditioning for Miami Vice," *AV Club*. Available at www.avclub.com/don-johnson-on-cold-in-july-dennis-hopper-and-auditio-1798269633.

Hill, Lee, *Easy Rider*. London: BFI Publishing, 1996.

Hinson, Hal, "Colors," *Washington Post*. Available at www.washingtonpost.com/wp-srv/style/longterm/movies/videos/colorsrhinson_a0c902.htm.

Holland, Frederick May, *Frederick Douglass: The Colored Orator*. New York: Haskell House, 1969.

Hopper, Dennis, Interview with Quentin Tarantino conducted by Dennis Hopper, "Blood Lust Snicker Snicker in Widescreen," in *Dennis Hopper: Interviews*, ed. Nick Dawson. Jackson: University Press of Mississippi, 2012.

Howe, Desson, "Hopper Marks 'The Hot Spot'," *Washington Post*. Available at www.washingtonpost.com/archive/lifestyle/1990/10/26/hopper-marks-the-hot-spot/267b629a-78af-410a-9303-3b76813ac0a0/.

Hundley, Jessica and Thomas, Pat, "Dennis Hopper's Legendary 'Last Movie' Finally Gets a Soundtrack Album, Five Decades Later, Via Record Store Day," *Variety*. Available at https://variety.com/2020/music/news/last-movie-soundtrack-record-store-day-vinyl-exclusive-dennis-hopper-1234752570/.

Jay-Z, *Introduction to Know What I Mean?: Reflections on Hip-Hop*. New York: Civitas Books, 2007.

Kalinak, Kathryn, *Film Music: A Very Short Introduction*. Oxford: Oxford University Press, 2010.

Kelly, Bill, "'Colors,' Controversy & Hopper in an Exclusive Interview – Dennis Hopper Discusses Colors, His Most Ambitious Filmmaking Venture Since Easy Rider, and Reflects on Three Decades of Acting," *South Florida Sun Sentinel*. Available at www.sun-sentinel.com/news/fl-xpm-1988-04-17-8801240357-story.html

King, James, "The Punishment Remains the Same – Reflecting on Dennis Hopper's The Last Movie," *HOME*. Available at https://homemcr.org/article/the-punishment-remains-the-same-reflecting-on-dennis-hoppers-the-last-movie/.

Kohn, Eric, "The Last Movie: Dennis Hopper's Misunderstood Masterpiece Deserves a Second Chance – and Now, It's Getting One," *Indiewire*. Available at www.indiewire.com/2018/08/the-last-movie-dennis-hopper-restoration-1201990114/.

Leary, Timothy, *Flashbacks Personal and Cultural History of an Era*. Los Angeles: J.P. Tarcher. 1990.

Luck, Richard, "A Reefer Runs Through It: The Making of Easy Rider," *Sabotage Times*. Available at http://sabotagetimes.com/reportage/a-reefer-runs-through-it-the-making-of-easy-rider/.

Margaritoff, Marco, "Inside the Text of Kurt Cobain's Heartwrenching Suicide Note," *All That's Interesting*. Available at https://allthatsinteresting.com/kurt-cobain-suicide-note.

Martin, Adrian, "The Misleading Man: Dennis Hopper," in *Stars in Our Eyes: The Star Phenomena in the Contemporary Era*, ed. Angela Ndalianis and Charlotte Henry. Westport: Praeger, 2002.

Maslin, Janet, "Taxidermy and Temptations: Dennis Hopper's Dark World," *New York Times*. Available at www.nytimes.com/1990/10/12/movies/reviews-film-taxidermy-and-temptations-dennis-hopper-s-dark-world.html.

Mastropolo, Frank, "How the Groundbreaking 'Easy Rider' Changed Soundtracks Forever," *Ultimate Classic Rock*. Available at https://ultimateclassicrock.com/easy-rider-soundtrack/.

Neild, Anthony, "Films for Music: Neil Young's Human Highway Reappraised," *The Quietus*. Available at https://thequietus.com/articles/11882-neil-young-human-highway-the-quietus-anthony-nield.

Orlean, Matthieu, "Photography, Writing, Acting . . . Movie-Making had Everything in One Package: Interview with Dennis Hopper," in *Dennis Hopper and the New Hollywood*. Paris: Flammarion, 2009.

Patrey, Jefferson, "Dennis Hopper's 'The Last Movie' at Northwest Film Forum," *Adventures in Sight and Sound Blog*. Available at https://blog.adventuresinsightandsound.com/2018/08/dennis-hoppers-last-movie-at-northwest.html.

Rochlin, Margy, "Stewart Stern Out of the Soul," in *Backstory 2: Interviews with Screenwriters of the 1940s and 1950s*, ed. Pat McGilligan. Los Angeles: University of California Press, 1997.

Rose, Aaron, "The Unvisual City," in *Dennis Hopper: Colors. The Polaroids*. Bologna: Damiani, 2016.

Rosenbaum, Jonathan, "Top Ten Lists 1974–2006," *Chicago Reader via Archive.org*. Available at https://web.archive.org/web/20110607040346/http://alumnus.caltech.edu/%7Eejohnson/critics/rosenbaum.html.

Rosenthal, Donna, "Hopper's Odyssey – From Hell to Texas: Dennis Hopper Has Experienced Acting Success, Druggy Exile, Psychiatric Wards and Now He's Directing 'Hot Spot'," *Los Angeles Times*. Available at www.latimes.com/archives/la-xpm-1989-11-05-ca-1727-story.html.

Sachs, Ben, "Dennis Hopper's Out of the Blue Remains a Powerful Depiction of Teen Delinquency," *Chicago Reader*. Available at https://chicagoreader.com/blogs/dennis-hoppers-out-of-the-blue-remains-a-powerful-depiction-of-teen-delinquency/.

Salinas, Ivan, "Easy Rider' in 2020: Born to Be Dead," *Daily Sundial*. Available at https://sundial.csun.edu/156233/arts-entertainment/easy-rider-in-2020-born-to-be-dead.

Sanchez, Rosa, "Police, Residents Plead for Ceasefire After South LA Sees 59 Shooting Victims in 1st 2 Weeks of 2021," *ABC News*. Available at https://abcnews.go.com/US/police-ceasefire-south-la-sees-59-shooting-victims/story?id=75441899.

Scharres, Barbara, "From Out of the Blue: The Return of Dennis Hopper," *Journal of the University Film and Video Association* 35, no. 2, Spring 1983. Available at www.jstor.org/stable/20686939.

Schneider, Daniel, "Convention Defiance in Dennis Hopper's Easy Rider," *Pop Matters*. Available at www.popmatters.com/dennis-hopper-easy-rider-defiance.

Soderburg, Brandon, "Dennis Hopper, Soundtrack Savant: The Unacknowledged Music Savvy Behind Easy Rider, Out of the Blue, and Colors," *The Village Voice*. Available at www.villagevoice.com/2010/06/01/dennis-hopper-soundtrack-savant-the-unacknowledged-music-savvy-behind-easy-rider-out-of-the-blue-and-colors/www.villagevoice.com/2010/06/01/dennis-hopper-soundtrack-savant-the-unacknowledged-music-savvy-behind-easy-rider-out-of-the-blue-and-colors/.

Stanislavski, Konstantin, *Stanislavski: An Actor Prepares; Building a Character; Creating a Role*. Abingdon: Taylor & Francis, 1989.

Stephens, Chuck, "Death's Angel: Peter Fonda in Easy Rider," *Criterion*. Available at www.criterion.com/current/posts/6572-death-s-angel-peter-fonda-in-easy-rider.

Stevens, Brad, "Dennis Hopper: The Last Director," British Film Institute: *Sight and Sound*. Available at https://www2.bfi.org.uk/news-opinion/sight-sound-magazine/comment/obituaries/dennis-hopper-last-director

Stewart, David, "Dennis Hopper's Blue Period: The Making of Out of the Blue," *Please Kill Me*. Available at https://pleasekillme.com/dennis-hopper-out-of-the-blue-1980/.

Thoret, Jean-Baptiste, "Dennis/Hopper, or the Man Who Was Two and One," in *Dennis Hopper & the New Hollywood*, ed. Matthieu Orlean. Paris: Flammarion, 2010.

Tracy, Andrew, "(En)fin de cinema The Last Movie," *Reverse Shot*. Available at www.reverseshot.org/symposiums/entry/235/last_movie.

Unknown author, "American Dreamer: A Look at Dennis Hopper," *Ransom Note*. Available at www.theransomnote.com/art-culture/reviews-art-culture/american-dreamer-a-look-at-dennis-hopper/.

Watson, Ben, *Honesty is Explosive!: Selected Music Journalism*. San Bernardino: Bongo Press, 2010.

Woodend, Dorothy, "Out of the Blue," *The Tyee*. Available at https://thetyee.ca/ArtsAndCulture/2010/11/12/OutOfTheBlue/.

Index

Alice's Restaurant 24
Almereyda, Michael 4, 8n4
Along For the Ride 68
Alonso, María Conchita 45, 53
American Dreamer, The 6, 24–5, 30–2, 70
American Friend, The 34, 67
Anderson, Stephen Milburn 46
Anspaugh, David 2, 44
Apocalypse Now 11, 30
"Are You Lonesome Tonight?" 39
Askew, Luke 14
Auster, Albert 32n1, 50, 55n14

"The Ballad of Easy Rider" 18, 20, 31
Band, The 14, 47
Barfly 64
Basil, Toni 17
Beat Generation, The 69
Beatles, The 3, 10, 12
Becker, Carol 32, 33n18, 33n20
"Be My Baby" 11
Benson, Sheila 50, 56n15
Bill Haley and His Comets 12
Blackboard Jungle 12
Black, Karen 17
Black Lives Matter 46
Black Panthers 3–4, 52, 69
Bleach 39
Bloodbath 67
Bloods 46
Blue Collar 60
Blues Brothers, The 62
Blue Velvet 2, 44, 67
Bogdanovich, Peter 65

Bonnie and Clyde 24
"Born to Be Wild" 11, 13–14
Boyle, Danny 11
Boyz n the Hood 46
Brando, Marlon 4, 36
Bringing It All Back Home 18
Buckley, Tim 69
Bujalski, Andrew 65
Bukowski, Charles 64
Burr, Raymond 35
Byrds, The 5, 10, 14, 18, 31, 47, 69
Byrnes, Jim 42

Cambern, Donn 12, 16
Carpenter, John 60
Carson, L.M. Kit 6, 30
Catchfire 4, 65, 67
CeBe Barnes Band 43
Chasers 4, 62, 64–5
Cheadle, Don 45
Chuck D 48
Clark, Gene 6, 31
Cobain, Kurt 39, 43
Colombier, Michel 67
Colors 3–4, 6–7, 45–54, 57, 62, 65–6, 68–70
"Colors" 49
Colors: The Polaroids 46, 55n9, 68
"Come as You Are" 39
Connelly, Jennifer 57–8
Conner, Bruce 3, 65, 70
Coppola, Francis Ford 4, 11, 44
Coppola, Sofia 65
Corman, Roger 4, 18, 21
Couleur Chair 34

Crash (TV series) 41
Crazy Horse 41
Crips 46
Crosby, Stills, and Nash 12
Crosby, Stills, Nash, and Young 41
Crowe, Cameron 65

Dahl, John 58
Davis, Mike 3, 7, 48, 55n11, 57, 59–61, 70
Day, Steve
Dean, James 1, 4
De La Manitou, Satya 68
Dennis Hopper: In Dreams: Scenes from the Archive. 68
"Don't Bogart Me" 15–16, 20
Doors, The 3, 11, 69
Dorham, Kenny 48
Do the Right Thing 46
Douglas, Frederick 11, 22n2
Drummond, Tim 7, 57, 61
Duvall, Robert 45, 50
Dylan, Bob 3, 5, 10, 12, 18, 20, 31, 69
Dyson, Michael Eric 54, 56n28, 56n29, 70

Easy Rider 2–5, 7–8, 10–23, 24–8, 30–2, 34, 36–7, 40–2, 47–8, 51, 53–4, 58, 60, 62, 64–70
Easy Rider 2: The Ride Home 64
"Easy Rider, 1970" 31
Ebeling, Nick 68
Ebert, Roger 26, 32n4
Electric Flag, The 10, 18
Electric Prunes, The 5, 10, 17, 69
Elliot, Cass 21
"The End" 11
Eric B. & Rakim 47

Fall, The 11
Farrell, Sharon 35
Figgis, Mike 57
Fisher, Mark 69, 70n3
"Flash, Bam, Pow" 18
Floyd, George 46
Fonda, Peter 2, 5, 10–11, 18, 20–1, 24–5, 68, 70, 70n4

Ford Cougar Advertisement 13
Ford, John 65
Forman, Miloš 60
Fraternity of Man 15–16
Frawley, James 35
Freedom 41

Gallo, Vincent 65
Garcia, Stella 25
Gehry, Frank 46
Glaser, Paul Michael 52
Glory Stompers, The 2, 22
Godard, Jean-Luc 65
Goldsmith, Jerry 47
Goodwin, Andrew 13, 23n7, 48, 55n10
Gordon, Don 26, 39
Graduate, The 12–13, 24
Guardians of the Galaxy 65

Hackford, Taylor 60
Hagedorn, John 48, 51, 54, 56n18, 56n25, 56n30
Hancock, Herbie 47–8
Hardin, Jerry 59
A Hard Day's Night 12
Hathaway, Henry 4, 6, 66
Hawker, John 59
Head 12
"Heartbreak Hotel" 38
"Heart Shaped Box" 39
Hell Hath No Fury 57
Hells Angels on Wheels 22
Hendrix, Jimi 10, 16–17, 20, 47
Heron, Gil Scott 69
Highsmith, Patricia 67
Hill, Walter 46
Hinson, Hal 45–6, 55n4, 55n8
Hired Hand, The 24
Holy Modal Rounders, The 5, 11, 15, 69
Holzer, Jenny 67
Homeless 67
Hooker, John Lee 7, 57, 59, 60–1
Hoosiers 2, 44, 47
Hopper/Welles 68
Hot Spot, The 4, 7, 42, 57–62, 65, 70
Hughes, Albert 46

Hughes, Allen 46
Human Highway 44
Hundley, Jessica 27–8, 33n12
Hunter, Tim 2, 44

Ice-T 47, 49
"If 6 Were 9" 16–17, 20, 47
"If You Want to Be a Bird" 15–16
Iggy and the Stooges 11
Indian Runner, The 3
"It's Alright, Ma (I'm Only Bleeding)" 18
"I Wasn't Born to Follow" 14, 20

Jagger, Mick 41
Jaglom, Henry 5, 12, 34, 65
Jarmusch, Jim 65
Jaws 6
Jay-Z 54, 56n27
Jefferson Airplane 21
Jesus's Son 1–2
Jimi Hendrix Experience 5
Johnson, Don 57–8
Jones, Nick 41
Jones, Spike 41
Joplin, Janis 20, 30
July, Miranda 43
Jungle Warriors 44

Kalinak, Kathryn 7, 9n6
Karr, Elizabeth 37
Kazan, Elia 65
Kerouac, Jack 69
Kid Blue 34
"Kill All Hippies" 43
King, Jr, Martin Luther 3–4, 20
King, Rodney 46
King of the Mountain 44
Kirkland, Sally 44
Klick, Roland 41, 44, 67
Kovács, László 5, 11, 14, 22, 26, 66
Kristofferson, Kris 6, 28–9, 30
Kubrick, Stanley 65
"Kyrie Eleison Mardis Gras (When the Saints)" 17

Landis, John 62
Lanza, Anthony M. 2, 22

Las Flores Del Vicio 34
Last Movie, The 2, 4, 6, 18, 25–32, 34, 37, 39, 42, 53, 66, 68, 70
Last Poets, The 69
Lavin, Tom 38
Leary, Timothy 11, 22n1
Lee, Spike 46
"Let's Turkey Trot" 16
Lewis, Paul 57
Linklater, Richard 37, 65
Little Eva 16
"Lonesome Traveller" 59
L'Ordre et la sécurité du monde 34
Los Lobos 47
"Love M. D." 59
Lucas, George 34
"Lust for Life" 11
Lynch, David 2, 4, 44, 58

Mad Dog Morgan 34, 67
Madsen, Virginia 57–8
Mahal, Taj 7, 57
Malick, Terrence 65
Mamas and the Papas, The 21
Manson, Charles 31
Manz, Linda 35
Martin, Adrian 2–3, 8n3, 22, 23n16
Marvel Cinematic Universe (MCU) 65
McGuinn, Roger 18, 20
MC Shan 47–8
"Me and Bobby McGee" 28, 30
Mean Streets 11
Merv Griffin Show, The 32, 33n19
Mickey One 24
"A Mind is a Terrible Thing to Waste" 48–9
Mirror Ball 41
Mission, The 47
Mitchell, Joni 20
Mitchum, Robert 57
Monk, Thelonious 48
Monkees', The 12
Mora, Philippe 4, 34
Morricone, Ennio 47
"My My, Hey Hey (Out of the Blue)" 36, 39, 42
"My Teddy Bear" 38

Nance, Jack 57
Narizzano, Silvio 67
Natural Born Killers 58
Nicholson, Jack 2, 5, 11–12, 15, 18, 21, 65, 68
Night Tide 2
Nitzsche, Jack 57, 60
No Way Out 52
N.W.A 3

Officer and a Gentleman, An 60
One Flew Over the Cuckoo's Nest 60
"One Time One Night" 47
Orange cell phone advert 64
Orlean, Matthieu 23n13, 29, 33n15
Other Side of the Wind, The 68
"Outlaw Song" 31
"Out of Luck" 40
Out of the Blue 2–6, 34–9, 41–3, 44, 53, 60, 62, 66, 68–70

Palmer, Earl 7, 57
Pearl Jam 3, 41
Penn, Sean 3–4, 45, 50, 64, 65
Perry, Alex Ross 65
Phillips, Michelle 21, 29–30
Pointed Sticks, The 40–1, 43, 66
Powell, Bud 48
Presley, Elvis 35, 38–9, 42–3
Primal Scream 43
Public Enemy 69
Puff Daddy 52–3
"The Pusher" 13

Rafelson, Bob 65
Ray, Nicholas 4, 25
Reagan, Ronald 3, 16, 36–7, 50, 64
Rebel Without a Cause 1, 25
Red Rock West 58
Reichardt, Kelly 65
Reitman, Jason 65
Reservoir Dogs 11
Reynolds, Simon 69
Rikert, Dustin 64
River's Edge 2, 44, 67
"Rock Around the Clock" 12
Rogers, Roy 7
Rolling Stones, The 3, 12, 60

Ronettes, The 11, 21
Rosenbaum, Jonathan 30, 43n6
Rotten, Johnny 36, 39, 42–3
Round Midnight 47
Rourke, Mickey 64
Rumble Fish 44
Running Man, The 52
Running Out of Luck 41
Rust Never Sleeps 41

Sadler, William 57
Salinas, Ivan 19, 23n14
Salt-n-Pepa 47, 53
Scharres, Barbara 27, 33n8, 33n10, 43n2
Schiller, Lawrence 6, 30
Schneider, Daniel J. 18, 23n10
Schrader, Paul 60
Schroeder, Barbet 64
Schwarzenegger, Arnold 53
Scorsese, Martin 65
"Screaming Metaphysical Blues" 31
Search and Destroy 3
Sevigny, Chloë 37
Sex Pistols 3, 36, 42, 69
Shaking the Cage 20
Shakur, Tupac 3, 55
Shanté, Roxanne 47, 53
Shelton, Lynn 65
Sikelianos, Chris 31
Silva, Trinidad 45
Simon and Garfunkel 12
Simon, John Alan 37
Simone, Nina 21
Sinatra, Nancy 21
Singleton, John 46
Slick, Grace 21
"Smells Like Teen Spirit" 39
Smith, Charles Martin 59
Sobel, Curt 67
Soderburg, Brandon 8, 9n9
"Somebody's Mom" 40
Sons of Katie Elder, The 25
"Sorry Just Won't Do" 42
South Central 46
Spector, Phil 10, 26, 60
Speed 3, 64
Spielberg, Steven 34

Squier, Billy 58
Starman 60
Star Wars 6, 35
Stealers Wheel 11
Steiger, Ueli 58
Steppenwolf 5, 10–11, 13, 69
Stern, Stewart 25–6
Stevens, George 66
Stills, Stephen 12
Stockwell, Dean 25
Stone, Oliver 58
Strasberg, Lee 1
"The Stroke" 58
"Stuck in the Middle with You" 11
Sub-Pop Records 39
Super Mario Bros 3

Tamblyn, Russ 25
Tarantino, Quentin 11, 65, 67
Tavernier, Bertrand 47
Thompson, Hunter S. 69
Tracks 5, 34
Tracy, Andrew 26, 32n6
Trainspotting 11
Trespass 46
Trip, The 18
Truffaut, François 65
Trump, Donald 16
Turner, Tina 20

Uneasy Rider 68
Universal Pictures 31

Van Sant, Gus 65
Vaske, Hermann 68
Vicious, Syd 35–6, 39, 42

Warhol, Andy 3, 65
Wasserman, Lew 31
Waterworld 3, 67
Watson, Ben 60, 63n4
Wayan, Damon 45
"The Weight" 14, 47
Welles, Orson 4, 65, 68
Wenders, Wim 4, 34, 67
"When the Saints Go Marching In" 17, 20
White Star 41, 44, 67
Wild Angels, The 21
Wild One, The 36
Wilkin, John Buck 6, 29–31
William, Charles 57
Williams, Jr, Hank 59
Williams, Roosevelt "Grey Ghost" 59

X, Malcolm 3–4, 69
XTRMNTR 43

Yakir, Leonard 6, 34
Yellow Submarine 12
Young, Neil 12, 36, 38–9, 41–3, 44, 60
"You're Nobody till Somebody Loves You" 59

For Product Safety Concerns and Information please contact our EU representative GPSR@taylorandfrancis.com
Taylor & Francis Verlag GmbH, Kaufingerstraße 24, 80331 München, Germany

www.ingramcontent.com/pod-product-compliance
Lightning Source LLC
Chambersburg PA
CBHW051759230426
43670CB00012B/2359